CHRIST'S PENOLOGY
AN APPLICATION OF
FORGIVENESS IN RESTORATIVE JUSTICE

John T. Krimmel, Sr.

Rylan

Published by Rylan Books
Ronkonkoma, NY 11779

ISBN 10: 1-60797-894-6

ISBN 13: 978-1-60797-894-7

Printed in the United States of America.

This book is printed on acid-free paper.

Print Number   5   4   3   2   1

Table of Contents

Chapter 1

Christianity and Forgiveness

The American legal system evolved from the Anglo-Saxton notion of law that was directly and indirectly promulgated through religious connections to the church. Prior to the Anglo-Saxton influence the Law of Moses (otherwise known as The Ten Commandments) served for centuries as the foundation for notions of right and wrong behavior and the concepts of punishments associated with the wrong behaviors. I agree that our American legal system is one of vast complexity and worthy of great praise from scholars, theologians, philosophers and the great thinkers and commenters and dissenters of our time. However, the complexities of our legal system, we still hold to the notion that our sense of right and wrong and they evolved from religious thought. I start my theses on legal forgiveness (This could be the Penology of Christ) at the beginning of Jesus's ministry. As you can see forgiveness is a central concept of Christian thought. Indeed, forgiveness may be the central focus of Christianity. And, clearly Christianity has had a major influence on the shape of our American legal system.

Let us begin with the New Testament and the Gospel of Matthew. According to Matthew's Gospel, Jesus begins his public ministry by calling together his first group of disciples and delivering to a large assembly his Sermon on the Mount. In his sermon, Jesus gives those gathered there directions for right living in the kingdom of God. To be great in God's kingdom, Jesus preaches, one must live by God's standards. This most holy sermon was given to show us how to live as faithful subjects in God's world. The crowd had gathered on the side of a mountain to hear the Messiah speak. Blessed are the merciful, for they will be shown mercy, Jesus said (Matthew 5:7). To Jesus the beatitudes mean more than a simple blessing.

They mean that those who follow these holy guidelines will find hope, joy and a deep happiness independent of outward circumstances. Jesus was illuminating the need for his followers to reflect humility and self-sacrifice in all matters. No longer will Jesus' followers adhere to personal traits of selfishness or pride. Nor will they lust for material things or power. Jesus knows that God's greatest prophets including Elijah, Jerimiah and Daniel were persecuted mainly because they were prophets. This knowledge shall serve to comfort those who decide to follow in Jesus' footsteps. Here, Jesus lays it out that we are to be merciful especially to those facing persecution. Just seven sentences into his sermon he preaches, "Blessed are the merciful, for they will be shown mercy." Jesus made it a point to include showing mercy in his inaugural sermon because the Romans despised pity. If people suffered, it was believed, it was because they deserved to suffer punishment. The practice of mercy now becomes clear. Mercy is a practice, not simply a sentimental feeling. If Christians have nothing to give a sufferer then they should pray. Being merciful will draw no harsh feelings from neighbors. Being merciful may even lessen the bitterness that has fallen on people.

Continuing on with the sermon, in verse 38 Jesus said, "You have heard that it was said, eye for an eye and tooth for tooth. But I tell you, do not resist an evil person. If someone strikes you on the right check, turn to him the other also." When we are wronged our first response is to seek revenge. But Jesus said we should do well to those who harm us. We should stop keeping score and begin to forgive and love. Instead of planning retribution, pray for those who are hurtful. In Jesus' day the world was under the rule of retaliation. The Mosaic Law, the Code of Hammurabi and the Roman law all required that the wrongdoer should get as good as he gave. Chris warns us against vengeance and vindictiveness.

Revenge is not sweet, despite the proverb. It is poisonous and it breeds strife in an endless circle. Only in God's hand is justice secure for He holds justice forever in love. According to Jesus it is more important to give justice and mercy that it is to receive it. By praying and being peaceful we can overcome evil and oppression with goodness and love. Jesus continues by saying we need to forgive if we expect to be forgiven. We should love our enemies and love our neighbors. We should bless those who curse us. God made us all and we should love all and everything that God created. Jesus is telling us to be perfect as the heavenly Father is perfect. Our reward will be a heavenly life. And we are instructed here that when we pray to ask the Lord to forgive our debts as we have forgiven our debtors.

In Matthew 18: 21-35, Jesus tells us the parable of the unforgiving debtor. "The Peter came to Jesus and asked," Lord, how many times shall I forgive my brother when he sins against me? Up to Seven times? Jesus answered, I tell you not seven times but seventy-seven times." In the parable Jesus tells of a servant who owes his master ten thousand talents. He was unable to pay so the master ordered the servant's wife and children to be sold in order to satisfy the debt. The servant begged for mercy and the master forgave the debt. Subsequently, the servant confronted another servant who owed him one hundred talents. The other servant begged for mercy but his pleas fell on deaf ears. The servant had the debtor put in jail. When the master heard of this injustice he had the servant tortured in prison "This is how the heavenly Father will treat each of you unless you forgive your brother from your heart." Matthew 18: 35. The rabbis of the time taught their followers to forgive people that offended them three times. Jesus, on the other hand, said that we shouldn't even keep track of how many times we should forgive.

We should always forgive those who are repentant, no matter how many times they ask for forgiveness. Jesus is teaching us in the parable that God has forgiven all of our sins and we should therefor forgive all that owe us.

The injuries we receive in life are miniscule when we compare that to what we owe God. How can we possibly calculate the level of our forgiveness or our indebtedness? And how can we possibly compare ours to God's? God's forgiveness of us is linked to our forgiveness of others. God is always ready to forgive but he cannot forgive a hardened heard, or an unforgiving heart. God is helplessly in love with us but he cannot forgive an unforgiving man. Many people complain that they don't feel God's mercy. Are they themselves forgiving? Moreover, we should be generously forgiving to others. Or else, we will face the consequences of living outside of God's law. In Luke 17: 3, Jesus said, "So watch yourselves, if your brother sins, rebuke him, and if he repents, forgive him. If he sins against you seven times in a day, and seven times he comes back to you and says, I repent, forgive him." In these cases forgiveness will help free your brother from his sin provided he repents and your rebuke is genuine and loving. Men can and should forgive. Man needs to dissolve all forms of resentment in prayer and learn to live alongside the offender in healing love. When men fail to pardon there becomes and endless circle of feud breeding more feud and bitterness bringing more bitterness.

In Mark 11:22-25, Jesus is explaining to his disciples the power of prayer. In v. 24 Jesus said, "Therefore, I tell you, whatever you ask for in prayer, believe that you have received it, so that it will be yours. (v. 25)

And when you stand praying, if you hold anything against anyone, forgive him, so that your Father in heaven may forgive you for your sins." Forgiving others is tough work. Many people simply cannot do it. Unforgiving people will stay separated from God.

When a person is praying and is simultaneously holding a grudge it is like a tree sprouting but not bearing fruit. Real forgiveness-filled prayer fills all the personal and secret holes of vengeance and pride with God's love. Moreover, true faith seeks justice and peace. Also, forgiveness brings harmony to a body of believers. Forgiveness allows people to let go of hurts, notions of suffering caused by others, and to release stubborn grudges. True believers forgive others. A church congregation of forgivers can literally change a neighborhood. A neighborhood filled with forgiveness can change a city, and a city filled with forgiveness can change a .... and so on. Jesus wants us to explore the unexplored power of prayer. There are no limits to the spiritual depths of prayer. Our faith in God can indeed change the world. Prayer provides man with a channel for the grace and power of God. To a great extent the measure of forgiveness we extend to others is a measure of the forgiveness we are capable of receiving. Forgiveness of sins by God can only be given to one prepared to receive it. The act of forgiveness cannot be bestowed on a person who has never experienced forgiving.

A person who says he forgives but does not forget does not know the true meaning of God's forgiveness. Keeping a grudge alive is like trying to hide something from God which is impossible.

The apostle Paul in his letter to the Romans (Romans 12: 9-21) writes that love must be sincere. Hate is evil; cling to what is good. Be devoted to one another in brotherly love.

Paul writes, "Bless those who persecute you; bless and do not curse. Do not repay anyone evil with evil. Do not take revenge, my friends, but leave room for God's wrath, for it is written, "It is mine to avenge; I will repay says the Lord. On the contrary, if your enemy is hungry feed him, if he is thirsty give him something to drink, in doing this you will heap burning coals on his head. Do not be overcome with evil but overcome evil with good." And in Ephesians 4:32 Paul writes, "Be kind and compassionate to one another, forgiving each other, just as in Christ God forgave you."

In the first chapter of Matthew, an angel came to Joseph. The angel said, "Mary is conceived in her from the Holy Spirit. She will give birth to a son, and you are to give him the name Jesus, because he will save his people from their sin. "God has planned from the beginning of time to forgive his people and release them from the guilt and stain of sin. And in 1 Peter, he writes, "rid yourselves of all malice and all deceit, hypocrisy, envy, and slander of every kind. Like newborn babies, crave spiritual milk, so by it you may grow in your salvation, now that you have tasted that the Lord is good. Do not repay evil with evil or insult with insult but with blessing, because this is what you were called so you may inherent a blessing.

Perhaps the most powerful example of such forgiveness is that of Jesus himself. "He came to his own people and his own people did not receive him"(John 1:12). His miracles and sermons attracted the crowds, but when he had to say some hard things, they would leave as quickly as they had come (John 6:66). Many people were aloof from Jesus. The resented him. They actively disliked him. A number of times, when he said something they didn't consider agreeable, they became upset and they tried to kill him, but he slipped away from their grasp. He came to his own home but people did not receive him. But Christ did rise above the anger of man. Jesus knew that he had the power to lift mankind to new a new level of evolution, to a new a more noble life, and to a scale never before seen. As often as people rejected Christ, he continued to find new creatures on the street willing to open their hearts to Him. The time finally came that God had planned (Galatians 4: 4-5).

Jesus knew it was coming, and though it filled him with pain to think of it, he faced it openly. This time when his enemies sought to arrest him, he stood forth, said "I am the man," and allowed them to take him. He allowed a mock trial filled with patently false and unsupported charges. He could have called legions of angels to deliver him. The armies of heaven were at his immediate disposal but he did not summon them. Soldiers spat in his face and mocked him with a cruel crown of thorns and a purple robe, which they said made him look like a king. They scourged him nearly to death. Pilate washed his hands and ordered his crucifixion. And as they crucified him, he said, "Father, forgive them, for they know not what they do."(Luke 23:34) If we are to know and understand God, we must love each other. We must know, accept and understand forgiveness. If we reject this part of God, we reject the kernel of who he is. Jesus puts it bluntly, you must forgive in order to be forgiven (Matthew 6:14-15).

Forgiveness is oftentimes very vexing. Maybe it is not too hard to forgive people we don't know. The people with whom we have a relationship of trust who turn on us, who betray our trust. Those people are the hardest to forgive. Husbands, wives, fathers, mothers, children, and boyfriends and girlfriends and our best friends. They can turn on us and wound us deeply. Sometimes we even doubt that, "It is better to have loved and lost, than never to have loved at all." Maybe we should withdraw and protect ourselves and never venture out again.

The path to good health is forgiveness. The path of healing is forgiving. True forgiveness does not minimize the sin or the hurt, nor excuse the sinner. True forgiveness chooses not to hold the sin against the sinner any longer. True forgiveness is a total and complete pardon. You may be freshly wounded and find your anger too massive to forgive. The injustice may be ongoing, the outrage constant. Perhaps you do not feel you are able to forgive right now. Then I ask you to pray this prayer: "Lord, I find it beyond my ability to forgive this person. I ask you to make me able to forgive in the future. You can find a most profound set of verses of the Bible appearing in Isaiah and John:

I revealed myself to those who did not ask for me; I was found by those who did not seek me. To a nation that did not call on my name, I said, 'Here am I, here am I. 'All day long I have held out my hands to an obstinate people, Who walk in ways not good, pursuing their own imaginations. A people who continually provoke me to my very face, offering sacrifices in gardens"(Isaiah 65:1-3) In spite of a history of insult and betrayal, "For God so loved the world, that he sent his only begotten Son, that whosoever believeth in him should not perish, but have everlasting life."(John 3:16)

God's initiative to be worshiped is disclosed over and over again the both the Old and New Testaments. The Lord laments, I am so with you and my love is unwearyingly divine, but you do not call my name. God waits to be gracious and asks only the confiding and obedient affection from us, His children. Jesus' demands for obedience and forgiveness of others should be viewed against this tapestry of God's persistent artful and steadfast love. Jesus tells those who will listen to him that forgiveness as a condition of entry into God's kingdom.

If we cannot forgive, or if we cannot understand forgiveness, then God's forgiveness of us Is not possible. We must forgive. We make all sorts of emotional excuses for ourselves. We find doctrinal reasons to set aside the clear teachings of our Lord and not take them seriously. But his words remain. Not forgiving is not an option for a Christian. We may struggle, we may not have the strength on our own and call out to Him for the will and the power to forgive, but we cannot hold onto our bitterness and simultaneously continue to hold onto him.

Do we have to forgive someone who does not repent? We read "If your brother sins, rebuke him, and if he repents, forgive him."(Luke 17:4) I think that forgiveness is something like a pardon. We have to accept it for it to be granted. In a technical sense, we can't really forgive someone who does not repent. But that doesn't let us off the hook. I think that God requires us to love our enemies, and this from our side of the relationship differs little from what forgiveness would require of us. In the Sermon on the Mount, Jesus is very clear, "I tell you: Love your enemies and pray for those who persecute you, that you may be sons of your Father in heaven.... Be perfect, therefore, as your heavenly Father is perfect."(Matthew 5:43, 48) Technical forgiveness, then, is not the issue, really. It is love from the heart that is what God requires of us. We are expected to love and forgive our enemies. Forgiveness is what flows from that kind of heart when there is repentance. Love must always flow. Not that any of this is easy. It can be heart-wrenchingly vexing. But discipleship is following and learning from Jesus. If we fail to learn this lesson of forgiveness and love our enemies, we miss the essence of God himself.

Why a New theory?

My most poignant recollection of the 2016 presidential debates were of the promises by both candidates to reform the criminal justice system. America, it seems, was in a terrible place with the increased violence against police officers and the simultaneously frequent occurrences of police officers fatally shooting suspects. At the same time America was suffering from a mass-incarceration malaise where the perception lingered that most of the incarcerated were people of color. It seems America was being besieged with violence. Accordingly, the American justice system overwhelmingly relies on prison as an option more so than any other country. With over 2 million people in prison, American has the highest incarceration rate in the civilized world, by far. Thus, the presidential candidates needed to say something as cities erupted in riots over this issue. "We need criminal justice reform" both candidates retorted. As we contemplate this rhetoric, we realize that American citizens are fearful of violent crime and criminals and many American citizens feel as though the response to crime is imbalanced and rests unfairly on the backs of black citizens, especially black men. So how does a society respond to random acts of violence? America responds with punishment. However, a dilemma occurs when a substantial portion of the society believes that the punishment response is unfair. Our current punitive criminal justice system is not rooted in society's vision. The harsh punishment response to offenders is not shared by our citizenry. We need criminal justice reform because the citizens of America are not in agreement regarding the punishment response.

The fact is we are a reactionary criminal justice system. Proportionately very little of what the criminal justice system does is focused on prevention.

When most of what the criminal justice system does is react to crime then it is easy to punish. Punishment becomes the penal response. In our case no other options exist but punishment. Punishment has become the penal panacea. Punishment is easy, forgiveness is difficult. Our system, being based upon violence, became a state system of last resort. The state, like a criminal, has lost its patience. The criminal is impatient and the criminal justice system is impatient. Therefore, punishment is the understandable response. Embedded in our society is the expectation for both the criminal and the criminal justice system is punishment. Punishment has become equated with justice. The public heaps their expectations onto the penal system. They do so even when they can't decide on what they want. Shall we punish? Shall we forgive? The public's minds are often unclear and many times they contradict themselves. It is the public that is inadequate, not the system. Even the science of criminology cannot agree on a theory. They cannot agree to a single causation of crime. The crime theories are pluralistic. The (literally) hundreds of crime theories cannot agree on causation, reform or solution. Indeed, most theories do not include adequate reform measures or solutions. Thus, the science of criminology and the citizens in America cannot agree as to how to respond. Should we be more flexible? Should we be more ridged? Some are forgiven. Some are punished. Therefore, the system is forced to become discriminatory. Punishment does not work.

It seems as though justice and public safety have overwhelmed any reasonable notions of debt forgiveness. We now live in a society where a persons' rights have become more important than mercy for those who deserve it or to justify helping the needy.

Kindness and benevolence have been left to the bureaucracies of the criminal justice system and decisions have become questionably unkind. Decisions based upon a calculous fraught with impersonal rapid-fire discretion are the norm. Notions of mercy nowadays are seen as threats to justice as justice, vengeance and punishment have become synonymous. Even though mercy is an agreed upon Christian virtue our present-day society has trepidation when asked to adhere to its tenants. Bibas (2016) notes in his review of The Decline of Mercy by Tuckness and Parrish that we now speak a language of "rights" rather than of mercy. Social programs have replaced church-based charity and "do-gooder" benevolence has supplanted mercy. Decisions about people's lives have become impersonal and largely bureaucratic void of kindness and empathy. If criminal justice actors appear merciful they appear weak. Tuckness and Parrish point out that mercy has been on a collision course with justice as far back as the middle ages. Then retribution was seen as essential with justice. Mercy was equated with the monarchy and seemed to some as being arbitrary. On the other hand, by insisting upon political equality, punishment and impartiality justice and punishment leveled out to a plane of fairness for all. No more benefit of clergy, if you will. Care for criminals and the poor fell to the domain of public institutions and no longer to the church. The government when charged with protecting rights and keeping empathy in check has become heartless toward criminals. Somehow our notions of charitable expressions toward the poor are now lost. Over centuries our current criminal justice system has evolved into a rule-based, structured and bureaucratic machine, thus missing the opportunity to simmer notions of mercy in the hearts of decision makers.

Americans have a complex notion of God when it comes to understanding forgiveness versus punishment. By the way, according to the research, religion is a salient feature in the lives of its citizens. Contrary to the secularization of similar industrialized countries Americans, almost overwhelmingly believe in God. In short, Americans are a religious people. Conversely Americans appear to be conspicuously punitive when it comes to notions of criminal justice. Many Christians fall along fundamentalist lines when it comes to discussion punishment. Religion for many people offers a rigid set of rules aligned with notions of Moses and The Ten Commandments. In a way, one can argue that religion fuels the flames of harsh views of punishment and the sinner. However Christian theology suggests that God takes part in a punishment outcome and, at the same time, offers forgiveness. God can be judgmental, punitive and forgiving and loving. Faith can have different effects on different people depending upon how their ethics are interpreted and imagined. It really depends on how we see God. If believers see God as a loving and forgiving counselor, then they are likely to believe less in the utility of punishment. God's mercy may become part of the formula for forgiveness on the criminal justice scales. A loving God, then, will show mercy. Can we?

Unnever, Cullen and Bartkowski (2006) present an article where they believe that the nature and intensity of a person's relationship with God creates a transportable cognitive schema that shapes their views toward punishment. In that article they present a theses that scholars believe that theories of punishment could benefit greatly if these theories included some aspect and recognition of the value of religion as citizens shape their attitudes toward punishment in the criminal justice system. They site Savensberg who writes, "the omission of religion from current theories of punishment is astounding."

Accordingly, the nature and intensity of a believer's relationship with God shapes the persons attitudes toward punishment. Greely (1995) posited an intensity or continuum of God's love starting with loving, intimate, and nurturing at one end and with distant, harsh and judgmental at the other. Greely labels his work as the "gracious image of God scale." This is instructive as we ponder both sides of a loving God and how these images shape attitudes toward punishment. The Bible offers us pretty clear guidance as to what camp God sides on regarding punishment. The Bible tells the readers that God wishes to have a personal and intimate relationship with His people. God is the world's creator and has formed with us a "covenant of love." God's love is merciful and forgiving and even more loving to those who repent. God's sense of brotherly love is an everlasting love. The Bible says God is love. People who view God in the aforementioned manner are more likely to exhibit love mercy toward others.

Suppose we developed a penology theory that considered the mystery of total love? Indeed, a criminal must be restrained but he also must be reformed. For the reform to occur we must see the criminal as a person. The loving parent can restrain the unruly child. Not only can the criminal justice system love the victims, they can also love the criminals. We shouldn't be forced to choose between the delinquent and the good citizen. In a loving penology paradigm all are equal. There is no discrimination. The mathematics of mercy equals forgiveness and it includes everyone. A theory based upon the teachings of Christ offers us a normative approach to penology and criminology and gives us a single way to respond to crime; with loving forgiveness.

The Intersection of Criminology and the Bible

The Bible has offered societies the roots of legal thought and the development of concepts of right and wrong from the beginning of time. It seems God has provided the citizens of earth a legal compass including definitions of right and wrong. For example, the Ten Commandments handed down from God to Moses served as the basis of such right and wrong behavior. In Exodus 20, Moses tells the citizens about the critical nature of the law of God. The law was intended to guide people as to how they should live. God gave his people the laws and guidelines for right living. The people learned the blessings of obedience and consequences of disobedience. Clearly, our laws today are based upon the laws of God. Moreover, the study of criminology and penology is concerned with those who break the law and how we might deal with the malfeasants (consequences). The law then becomes a necessary component to study criminals and their fates. In order to study law breakers we need to comprehend the law. Thus, criminology is directly linked to the Bible. Some may argue the linkage is not necessary for a discussion of science but one cannot deny the foundational nature of our legal and penal systems. Indeed, the first penitentiary in America, the current Eastern State Penitentiary in Philadelphia, was designed by religious leaders to foster Biblical respect and repentance.

The Bible is the best law book available to study the history of punishment. In Geneses 39:30, 40:5 the Bible tells a story where Joseph, a slave, was elevated to an important position in the household of the Egyptian, Potiphar. Potiphar trusted Joseph in all matters pertaining to his house. Potiphar's wife took notice of Joseph and she attempted to seduce him.

Joseph rejected her sexual advances and was ultimately imprisoned based upon testimony of the requited wife. Joseph was put into a prison, a place where the King's enemies were housed. It was a grim place with vile conditions. Joseph spent two years in that prison. He was eventually freed to interpret the dreams of the king.

In Judges 16:22 Sampson was imprisoned after Delilah saw to his shaving of his hair. Once the Lord left Sampson, he was subject the whim of the Philistines. They seized him, gouged his eyes out and bound him with shackles binding him to prison and punishment. The Old Testament contains sixteen instances of prison. Adam and Eve were banished and Cain and Abel wore marks of punishment. In the books of Ruth, 1 Samuel and 2 Chronicles the primary punishments were death and exile. The book of Ezra contains language of enforcement of religious regulations. Ezra called for death, banishment, confiscation of property and imprisonment for disobedience of the law. The first books of the Bible also illuminate covenants with God and his people. In Exodus 19 God tells Moses to obey him fully and keep his covenant, then out of all nations you will be my treasured possession. And in Exodus 20 God tells Moses of the Ten Commandments. In Deuteronomy 4, Moses tells his people to follow the covenant of God and that the people were to follow the laws of God. The people were expected to walk in the way of the Lord. The Old Testament contains over 600 pages of violence. One hundred Bible verses contain language where God explicitly commands somebody to commit violence for no apparent reason. The Old Testament is loaded with references to scapegoating and vengeance.

Also, animal sacrifice is never far from human sacrifice. However, Amos pointed out the priority of doing justice over engaging in worship and Hosea questioned punishment toward a balance of mercy and justice.

Embedded in the history of the Bible are accounts of life in Rome. Rome was founded in 735 BC and was initially ruled by kings. It became a republic in 509 BC. By 312 BC Rome was ruled by a single person. Constantine was the emperor. Under Constantine the law took the form of 12 tables. The laws were to rule over private matters and disputes. But private disputes did carry punishments including death, precipitation (throwing people to their deaths from high cliffs), hanging and decapitation. Incarceration was reserved for debtors. Rich people build private jails to house recalcitrant slaves and other enemies. Law was initially for private concerns but Rome was often under the uneasiness of social upheaval and violence served to expand the use of the law by the authority of the emperor. The emperor Augustus (31 BC - 14 AD) employed the highest punishment including crucifixion for horrendous offenders, especially those who questioned the authority of the emperor. Augustus threw people into the arena with beasts or burned the accused publicly. It was thought that aggravated punishments demonstrated the power of the emperor. Augustus appeared to have unlimited power and he unleashed it willingly. The history of punishment is mostly oral. Early historians report the chaining of prisoners as this act was depicted in plays. The convicted may have been sentenced to hard labor and slavery in a stone quarry. The military employed torture for violators including the use of deep cisterns. The Romans suspended law for serious crimes like treason or sorcery and their largest threat came from Christians. These accounts appear in the Gospels, and Epistles.

As you can see the Bible offers us a rich history of law, punishment, social control, and issues facing the oppressed. It is somewhat evident that under God's covenant people were on an honor system where obedience was rewarded with the love of God. It was the emperors of Rome that stretched the law into devices of their own gain. They believed they were gods and they deserved all the privileges of such a godliness.

The Ethos of the Christian religion

Forgiveness is central to Christianity. For Christians the concept of divine forgiveness, mediated through humans is one form of the love that should characterize the full life in the community and beyond. Humans learn forgiveness from each other thus creating a god-like behavior that becomes cultural. The Christian ethos is "if I forgive I can be like God." In the New Testament forgiveness always leads to reconciliation and reconciliation results from mutual experiences of forgiveness. Accordingly, Martin Luther wrote (Marty 1998) , "As tightly as the pedals of a rosebud, adhere to a common center, and radiate out like the rays of the sun from one glowing core, namely the gospel of the forgiveness of sins." Forgiveness remains as a guiding principle in Christian's lives. It is an honored tradition. Many use forgiveness as a plumb for complex traditions. In other words, forgiveness is the normative behavior. One that should be emulated by other religions. The religions of the world should be judged based upon the degree to which they forgive. Being religious and forgiving offers us a way to bring us into harmony. The ethos asks us to seek to change from being unforgiven and unforgiving to forgiven and forgiving. Being religious offers our culture a balancing beam of forgiveness. Is forgiving a right and or an obligation? Perhaps forgiveness is both.

The Christian reality is that God forgives and humans forgive. Sooner or later you have to say the word "god" in the respect to the theme of forgiveness.

In Exodus 34: 6-7, God appears to Moses and discloses divine ethos as, "abounding in steadfast love and faithfulness, keeping steadfast love for the thousandth generation, forgiving inequity and transgression of sin." Therefore, forgiveness by God, as a theme, appears early and is consistent. God wants to forgive. Kierkegaard (in Abrahamson 2010) said, "The most miraculous achievement of the Holy One is that He could forgive a sinner and make a new creation out of the fallen one." Central to Christian ethos are the following activities; confession, prayer, preaching, sacraments, justice and mercy (this is us in criminology). Jones (1995) said, "God's love moves us toward reconciliation by means of costly forgiveness." Humans are called to be holy by embodying forgiveness through specific habits and practices that seek to remember the past truthfully, to repair brokenness, to heal divisions, and reconcile and renew relationships. We see one God in a dynamic relationship of self-giving, self-receiving and perpetually giving love.

The Bible gives man the authority to forgive In Matthew 9:2-8 where it reads, "Take heart, son. Your sins are forgiven." And, "The son of man has authority on earth to forgive sons." We see the Bible says that humans can model divine forgiveness and therefore, humanistic forgiveness becomes a Christian ethos. In the Gospel of John, Chapter 20 verses 22 – 23 it reads, "And when he had said this, he breathed on them and said, receive the Holy Spirit. If you forgive the sins of any, they are forgiven them; if you withhold the forgiveness from any, it is withheld." Not only is forgiveness a Christian ethos, to not forgive is an equal action but in the opposite direction. In Matthew 3: 13-15 the Gospel says,

"Then Jesus came from Galilee to the Jordan to be baptized by John. But John tried to deter him, saying, "I need to be baptized by you, and do you come to do me?" Jesus replied, "Let it be so now, it is proper for us to do this to fulfill all righteousness." Then John consented. Baptism connects the believer to Christ. He accepts a newness of life. A life of forgiveness. Baptism and forgiveness are the keys to heaven. Forgiveness as a community is an ancient Christian theme. Community forgiveness helps us cope with troublesome and collective guilt as to our legacy of slavery, Native Americans or the Holocaust. Embodying forgiveness is the only way to effectively deal with awful events. Collectively we ought to focus on reconciliation of brokenness and the restoration of the community with God and the whole of creation. Forgiveness is then embodied in the center of Christian life.

Forgiving is steeped in religious thinking. The Prayer of Saint Francis Assisi reads, "Where there is hatred ley me sow love, where there is injury pardon. For it is in giving that we receive and in pardoning where we are pardoned. Buddha reportedly said "For hatred cannot put an end to hatred. Love alone can." Forgiveness in the religious context has allowed people to reduce conflict, fear, anger and estrangement. Forgiveness remains a mainstay of compassion, mercy and humility. But note, seeking forgiveness for yourself through a religious person is not the same as forgiving somebody else that offended you. In the religious context people are mostly seeking forgiveness through God. Forgiveness is learned through prayer, meditation, instruction and parable. In Judaism forgiveness is a religious obligation. It is even codified. In Tibet, the monks pray, "Remember the good things you have done, forgive everyone else in life, and ask forgiveness from anyone you have harmed." The Lord's Prayer asked for forgiveness for those who trespass against us.

Think about the secular world for a moment. What about the self-help industry? This industry tries to help their readers manage shame, guilt, grief, depression, and forgiveness.

Forgiveness is a response to wrongdoing and it can only take place if a moral offense actually takes place. We can see just how complex the definitions of moral offenses can be as are the complexities of responses to said moral offenses. But wrongdoing must be negligent, reckless or willfully wrong. Sometimes there a victims of a wrongdoing who have no idea they were wronged. But forgiveness is still needed. So, who can forgive? A direct victim of an offense is a primary victim. They immediately feel the impact of the wrong. A secondary victim is the family or friend or he wronged. And the tertiary victim is the affected community. Resentment also has three levels, primary, secondary and tertiary. Regardless of the type of victim or the type of resentment, nobody can forgive somebody else on behalf of somebody else. A victim mat feel the need to forgive but the secondary and tertiary victims may not support such an action. This can make the forgiveness act extremely complicated. Since forgiveness is a virtue, it not should be motivated by the desire to free oneself from guilt or shame. Forgiveness should be other-directed and never self-directed. As we mature our goal is to cultivate attitudes that we find morally worthy. But not goal seeking for forgiveness is often times one of trial and error. If a victim seeks counseling this may be the first step toward seeking a fellow human as warranting respect and compassion. Compassion is necessary but the victim should never feel superior to the offender. In the end, if we choose to forgive, we choose to see the wrongdoer as a person who warrants respect, requires compassion and our goodwill.

When we forgive and do not forget the incident, at least we no longer remember it with vindictiveness. We should begin to view the incident with objectiveness. When we forgive we make peace with the past and no longer need to concern ourselves with it. Genuine forgiveness can be difficult. It requires one to let go of anger and recover self-dignity.

It requires reconciliation. Moreover, it requires compassion, understanding and trust. Reconciliation is restoration of acceptance, benevolence and harmony.

Sometimes a relationship has to end for restoration to be complete. This may be the case in a past violent relationship. Reconciliation can occur but there should not be an expectation of restoration of the relationship. Some theorists believe that punishment and restitution are part of the forgiveness milieu. Punishment and restitution may be required if doing so will lessen the chances future harm will come to others. However, many believe that punishment is incompatible with the true meaning of forgiveness. Saying, "I forgive you," sometimes is true but saying it does not guarantee an absence of bitterness. Forgiveness requires behavior consequences.

Forgiveness and Religious Coping

Have you ever heard of the law of the instrument? It goes something like "If you had a hammer in your hand you're more likely to see nails all around you." Forgiveness then is either a religious pursuit or a method of coping. Or, perhaps both. Maybe the act of forgiving will feel right religiously and psychologically. Then you will see forgiveness as an option like you see those nails all about. When we find ourselves in a situation where we need to cope we are actually seeking significance in stressful times.

Significance, however, is both objective and subjective. Subjectively is like caring or feelings that we cannot explain and objective significance is like things which are more psychological and definable. Significant objects are not necessarily good. They can be relationships gone bad, abuse of alcohol or drugs are seeking social status at the expense of others. We find ourselves in coping situations when we try to hold on to things that require a subjective measure of value.

We need to hold onto things or we try to transform them. Coping involves the steps that help us to deal with a challenge or threat to things we value. If things are difficult we first turn to conservational coping methods. We try to hold on to the things we value. If the conservational coping methods fail we turn to transformational. We try to shift to entirely new objects of significance. First we try to change those objects of value. Then we try to transform them (or ourselves) into something else. Transformational coping calls for prayer, psychotherapy or rituals, like formal grief processes. Transformation is difficult. We often do this when everything else had failed. Forgiving is a form of forgiveness. Especially in cases of situations involving abuse, betrayal or victimization.

We may opt to conserve our old ways of thinking. Conservation gives us justice and is self-focused. Transformation gives us peace. When we conserve we cope through anger, fear, hurt and resentment. To transform we cope through reframing, humanizing, empathizing, reappraisal and social facilitation. Forgiveness gives us peace of mind and peace with others. Forgiveness requires us to change, cognitively, affectively, rationally, behaviorally, and spiritually. Forgiveness allows us to cope. It allows for emotional venting, changing of attitudes toward the wrongdoer and the victim and empathy toward the offender.

It reverses the negative effects of not forgiving. A spiritual life, filled with forgiveness, can be a way of life. Yours can be a life filled with anticipatory coping that allows one to preempt mistreatment. A life where one could never really be a victim. Spirituality is the greatest of human capacities and forgiveness is a serious religious pursuit. Religions offer the world ways to come to grip with our most terrifying problems. It always seeks new significance when old ones no longer seem tenable. Religion offers people new perspectives.

Forgiveness can be a method of religious transformation. Every religion places value on love, compassion and kindness. At the same time they also warn of the unbridled emotions of hatred and bitterness. In Colossians 3:13 "Christ forgave you, so also you do ye." Religious people place great value on forgiveness. Forgiveness is akin to a sacred quality. For example, married couples who take forgiveness to the sacred level live lives of harmony and mutual problem solving. We are all fundamentally human in spite of our differences and behaviors. Religion offers us a way to forgive. Joseph, Hosea and Christ. Religion offers us a world of forgiveness. Father forgive them. Forgiveness is placed higher on a spiritual context than hope, surrender and goodwill, Forgiveness is aligned with purity and forgiveness is a gift from God.

The most common act of forgiveness is asking God for forgiveness. Wrongdoers pray to God to forgive them and that the person they wronged also forgives them. Forgiveness is inseparable from religion. To consider forgiveness in a secular fashion might be considered an oxymoron. What other social institution is based upon forgiveness?

There is no single key for coping with strife. We know forgiveness is available option for coping but not everybody is ready or willing to forgive. A violation may be too fresh or severe. The victim may be still in treatment. Some people hold on to their pain in order to re-visit it or to constantly share it with others. Maybe their pain offers them a key to their life's significance. Forgiveness must consider justice, fairness and equity and we should not vie for forgiveness without paying attention to these concerns. When forgiveness is out of balance with the values of responsibility and justice it may be harmful. The cool thing about religion is that it offers resolve for problems outside of psychology. Religion has its own language. It is a language of surrender, letting go, conversion, faith, suffering, meaning, hope and forgiveness.

Religion speaks to our human frailty and morality. Studying forgiveness may offer the building of a bridge between religion and psychology. Interestingly, social science is on the brink of building new theoretical models of forgiveness. Forgiveness is a nascent social science. The new work in this science is looking at religion in terms of how it contributes toward forgiveness, imitating God for example. Religion can also offer us a world view of forgiveness but most research on forgiveness has been done in the confines of Christianity.

The Spiritual Roots of Restorative Justice

How does society deter crime, maintain public safety and make certain offenders pay? Remember, Americans cannot agree to this issue. People say we're too soft on crime and at the same time they say we're too hard on crime. Some claim criminals must be sick. Or, criminals are criminally insane. And mostly, nowadays we ignore victims. Arguably, people tend to form opinions about justice and punishment based on emotional standpoints. Many people base their opinions on horrific cases. The news media showers us with crime stories pretty much around the clock.

It is the extraordinary crimes that mold public reaction and sometimes subsequent legislation responses. Our legislators tend to craft crime policy based upon the worst case scenarios. The worst-case scenarios provide Americans with a common argot, a crime argot. This is dangerous. We currently see the mass-incarceration morass we are in because of hardline responses to extraordinary crimes. There has been a grass-roots movement in Canada, Australia and other countries to question sentencing policies. Restorative justice is asking for crime policies that include compensation for victims, reconciliation with the offender and restoring just order.

Restorative justice advocates raise fundamental concerns about criminal justice and question how punishment protects citizens' moral order, ensures offenders receive just deserts, and how well it serves to reform. Traditional theories of punishment fall into one of five categories; retributive, utilitarian, rehabilitative, restitution or restorative. Retributive is the oldest theory and is based upon notions of the Bible like an eye for and eye and vengeance.

Punishment must include pain, suffering and even death. Pain is justified in this model as the point is to right the wrong of the offender through punishments of deprivation, demoralization and dehumanization. These is no interest in treating the offender under the retributive model. Utilitarian theory is a 19th century concept and it was based upon the principle that punishment protected society from wrongdoers. Punishment is justified as it provides deterrence and adherence to the law. The difference between utilitarian and retributive models is that utilitarian thinking supported the idea that punishment should fit the crime. There was a growing opposition to harsh public punishments like beatings and hangings. Where les harshness may have resulted the expectation of a deterrent effect really had no mechanism for correcting the wrongs of an offender.

Deterrence theory require quick capture and subsequent punishment. The problem was just how much punishment was of utility. Rehabilitation theory considers crime to be an illness and it can be treated like a sickness. Rehabilitation theories were born from the growth of social sciences. Prisons became reformatories or correctional facilities. They were eventually seen as being too soft on criminals. Restitution theory concerns itself with paying back the victim monetarily. It is tied to minimalistic state theories in economics and political science. Here, they believe that governments should intervene as less as possible. The problem is this theory assumes victimization can be quantified monetarily and it assumes every wrong has a monetary value and wrongs can be solved. Finally, restorative justice seeks to find ways to resolve conflicts with minimal use of force.

Restorative justice ideologists believes that criminal justice should find ways to ameliorate conflicts in a legal way. If done right, restorative justice can restore justice, offer deterrence, rehabilitate and provide restitution. Critics say that just deserts and vengeance are embedded into American culture. Restorative justice offers us a way to do justice right but it faces significant resistance from the law and order community.

In Charles Wesley's journal of 1738 he noted the reign of Henry VIII saw 78,000 hangings. It was a very popular method of execution. Christianity has also its own history of violence. How do we reconcile this? Rene' Girard (1987) points out that the scapegoat mechanism is present in all cultures. It works unconsciously in cultures through rituals, rites and sacrifices. People revel during executions. Could this be the central anthropological issue of our age? Today a tiny amount of offenders bear the brunt of the death penalty as the serve as collective scapegoats for society. Christianity is based upon the victim of the death penalty. Jesus's penalty. Society was morally shaken after his death. It is time for another anthropological shift.

In John 16:3 the Bible reads, "For God so loved the world that he gave his one and only son, that whoever believes in him shall not perish but have eternal life." In Matthew 5:19 Jesus says, "But go and learn what this means, I desire mercy not sacrifice. For I have not come to call the righteous but sinners." There is tension between the love of God and vengeance. Vengeance and wrath are variable but God's love is constant. The words retribution and punishment have no place in the Christian vocabulary. God has liberated us from his punishment. Jesus is determined to disarm every executioner and set every prisoner free. In Luke 4 the Bible reads, "He has sent me to proclaim freedom for the prisoners and recovery of sight for the blind, to set the oppressed free and proclaim the year of the Lord's favor."

Jesus said in Matthew: 38-48, "If anyone slaps you on the right cheek, turn to them the other cheek. Jesus is asking us to love our neighbors. His message is that God is so completely loving and there are no strings attached. His love is a gift. It is not earned it is given. Jesus is offering us hope, fellowship and new beginnings. Forgiveness is the most significant process for overcoming the devastation of crime. Forgiveness brings together truth, forbearance, empathy and commitment to repair fractured relationships. Christ forgiving died on the cross forgiving criminals. This links criminology to Christ forever. Forgiveness liberates us from crime. The love of God and the ethos of forgiveness is the criminology of Christ. Restorative justice calls for communities to come together in acceptance and reconciliation in order to become communities committed to justice in a world of injustice.

Chapter 2

The Philosophy of Forgiveness

The literally hundreds of crime and criminology theories that we refer to cannot agree on causation, reform or solution. Indeed, most theories do not include adequate reform measures or solutions. Thus, the science of criminology and the citizens in America cannot agree as to how to respond to crime and criminals. Should we be more flexible? Should we be more ridged? Due to this lack of agreement regarding what to do to treat crime and criminals some are forgiven and some are punished. Therefore, the system is forced to become discriminatory and punishment becomes the default. However, we do know that punishment does not work. Perhaps, the most influential mentor regarding synthesizing complex theories was the writer of The Perennial Philosophy. Aldous Huxley (1945) pondered the multi-faceted nature of religious theories across the broad spectrum of the major religions of the world. I'll come back to this later and argue that the same methodology employed by Huxley might be appropriately applied to the science of criminology.

Huxley set out to discover the highest common factor in all preceding and subsequent theories of religion. He analyzed theoretical tradition, particular points of view and memorable parts of religions and philosophies. In Huxley's The Perennial Philosophy anthology he developed "one divine reality." As he examined texts he looked for the wonder boys of religious tradition and thought. He pondered, who are the saints, the prophets, sage ones, and the enlightened of the theories. What were these great thinkers thinking? What concepts were sacred to their theories? He was looking for the person who had already figured this out. And to that person, what did things matter? Huxley believed that the best we can do is study the works of all those who had figured out the connections of knowledge to human kind.

Huxley, after his study, concluded that the ultimate reason to be on earth is to serve god. According to philosophers, this is what all religions have in common and this is what connects people to reason. God gives people the capacity to reason through free will. The truth in the religious world is that we all should be striving to serve god, though diminishing the value of ourselves. God is love and is perfect. Love raises us up and gives us the motive to find god. For example, one way the find love is through works of charity. And to be truly charitable we need to lose feeling of craving, self-interest, egotistical thinking, wishing and acting. After all, we seek a means to an end through love and charity which is heaven.

The present exercise is not in any way meant to replicate the work of Huxley, but I did collect some information on the major religions of the world with an eye toward how different religions view forgiveness as an act of charity, or at least an act connected to the pleasing of their god. By the way, the majority of the peoples living on this earth believe in a god, in one form or another. The major religions of the world are Christianity, Buddhism, Islam, Hinduism and Sikhism. We discussed Christianity and forgiveness in Chapter One.

Buddhism (Loy 2001) has four major truths. First, life is duhkha (or unhappiness). Second, duhkha is caused by selfish cravings. Third, the end of duhkha is the destruction of craving and the fourth is the destruction of duhkha comes by following an eightfold path. The Buddhist is expected to life an eightfold path that include right understanding, right intention, right speech, right conduct, right vocation, right effort, right mindfulness and right concentration. These right paths offer guidance as to living properly in the eyes of Buddha. To the Buddhist, criminals exist because there is too much poverty. It is an obligation, therefore, to make sure no poverty exists in the neighborhood.

Poverty is the root cause of crime including theft, immoral behavior, engaging in telling falsehoods and violence. This problem begins when the rich (the king) does not give enough money to the needy. The Buddhists realize that crime and disorder cannot be separated from justice and the social order. Harsh punishments, they believe, contribute nothing toward the meeting peoples' basic needs. People should not be made to live in fear of law. Society should be able to live sufficiently without committing crimes.

Buddhists know that punishment is a mirror image of itself thus reinforcing the punitive actions. So, they know that violence begets violence. Therefore, violence can never result in peace. The religion has rules against killing, stealing, improper sexual conduct and using intoxicants. In fact, Buddhists believe that the root of all evil is lust, malice and the resultant delusion that it's ok to commit such acts. As long as people remain unenlightened there will be crime and violence. Buddhists believe that they should strive for behavioral perfection practice tolerance and be compassionate. The Buddhist must find ways to shift their focus away from punishment toward reformation as vengeance may result in bad karma and the recipient will inherent an evil life. Where forgiveness is not necessarily spelled out in religious dogma of Buddhism, compassion and justice certainly is. For the Buddhist, vengeance must be replaced with compassion.

In Islam the law is promulgated by God through the Qur'an. Legal codes are derived from sacred sources but interpreted by men. Thus, crime and punishment lies in the interpretive world of men. But guided by God in the Qur'an. For Islam's members are obligated to serve god and his creation. In god's creation crime is an abrogation of one's individual obligation to god.

According to Ammar (2001) the past quarter century Islam has turned to punitive methods. They have engaged in extreme miscarriages of justice that are associated with maldevelopment, inequity, increased poverty and marginality, lack of democratic dialogue, deteriorating educational systems, fewer employment opportunities and disparity caused by oil rich countries and other Muslim nations. In fact, however, the Qur'an contains a message of mercy and forgiveness. For them, God (Allah) is most forgiving. He forgives all sins for those who seek forgiveness. Allah is forgiving and most merciful. In the Islamic community a criminal is seen to disrupt the harmony of the neighborhood. The community is God's creation, after all. But, if a criminal is to be punished he is never to be disrespected. A criminal is never to be demonized for his crimes.

Islam contains many restorative justice components including mercy and forgiveness. In fact, crime classifications include the definitions of relationships between the offender and the victim as well as the community. The forgiveness of offenders is not an alien concept for the people of the Islamic faith. The law is so strict that citizens often agree to forgive the offender and lessen the charges. Moreover, Muslim communities often put into practice forms of forgiveness as they use mediation, arbitration and compensation as alternatives to punishment by their criminal justice system.

In Hinduism, social, moral, religious and natural laws are combined in a system of values known as Dharma (Neufeldt 2001). Dharma is expressed in a system of principles, regulations morality and laws of nature. The laws associated with Dharma are meant to guarantee the well-being into the next life. The religious principles foster a belief that people are obligated to bear the fruit of their actions and that their actions have consequences.

Dharma is related to follower's' obligations and duty to participate in religious rituals, caste duties, and commands and prohibitions as proscribed by law. In Hinduism the social milieu is defined by the caste system. Most law reflects neglect of duties as expected by the caste system.

People who follow the dharma put themselves on a oath to liberation or salvation. To beak the law is to pit oneself against the divine order. If a man sins he will bring misfortune against his children. Sin will bring unhappiness to all subsequent births. Plus, positions on life are dictated by your caste and dharma is the law of moral consequence. Most personal misfortune, it is believed, is inherited. In Hinduism, punishments for law violators are a divine necessity and punishment is only necessary for those who continue to break the law. Wise men know the dangers of the rod but to not punish can bring cosmic disorder. The king maintains the right to punish in the name of the divine. This system relies upon fines and compensation to victims. The lower casts suffer harsher punishments. The reincarnated (twice born) receive lesser punishments.

Hinduism calls for retribution against an offender. It is their classical response to crime. Retribution is necessary to restore order and helps to stabilize society. It also helps the victim. Hinduism is also very concerned with restoration to the victim. Punishment is justified as a way to cleanse the soul from its sin and an offender can go to heaven if his soul is clean. Ancient Hinduism calls for reparation to the offender. An apology restores the system's order. A return to the balanced social order requires restoration to the victim. This will return the victim and the offender to their places in the social order. It is believed that penance can remove he taint of sin. When sinners pay their dues past deeds are taken care of.

Hinduism sees the truth as being in the hearts of people practicing non-violence and service to all mankind. Victims and orphans should be served by others as we are all children of God. Penance and restitution are powerful cleansers and ultimately frees offenders and restores victims. Penance and restitution can remove the ugliness and taint of past offences.

According to Singh (2001) Sikhism is a system of culturally accepted gurus. The Guru Nanuk is the true king as he created the world. Guru Nanuk sits alone observing all and he dispenses true justice. The lord of true, his justice is true, and truth will be his judgement. God delivers faultless justice. His divine justice takes into account virtue and vice. It is part of god's judgement to include notions of forgiveness and tolerance. God's unlimited grace stresses to values of mercy, compassion and benevolence by the justice system. The system believes that we should strive to not deprive the rights of others. A violation of human rights can be considered more serious that the original offense. The Sikh view of justice contains two characteristics, respect for rights and non-exploitation of others. Brotherly love rises from proper acts of justice in such a manner that includes both justice and transformation of the offender that is consistent with the spiritual unity of all humankind. In this instance, forgiveness is a prized virtue and part of spirituality. Without forgiveness a vast number of people with much goodness would have perished form this earth. Forgiveness results in pure joy and a live of truth. The unforgiving are tyrants who cannot cultivate the virtue of forgiveness. They are humbled in dust and never reach the level of glory found in forgiveness. A forgiving person realizes to necessity vows of purity, a noble way of life and contentment. A forgiving man is immune from the maladies and malice of life. Forgiveness needs to be struggled for every day. It needs to be won on a daily basis. This is done through prayer as they strive for a spiritual life.

Self-centeredness is the main obstacle to forgiveness. Lust, covertness, attachment to worldly things and pride are powerful impulses that push people toward self-gratification. Prayer can ease the pain caused by self-gratification and self-centeredness. Prayer can cultivate such virtues as patience, charity, contentment and forgiveness. Forgiveness, mercy, compassion and understanding help to facilitate reconciliation. True forgiveness only occurs when we see the offender in a new light. We learn to see the offender as being vulnerable and we see his crimes as being an event unrelated to future drama. A mutual healing manifests between the offender and the community. People who hate others burn themselves on a fire of revenge. They never regain a true peace of mind. Our fight against evil can only be won with good, never evil against evil. Sikhism emphasizes mutual coexistence, tolerance, acceptance of others and their faiths, universal brotherhood, concern for the world community, liberty, and equality of race and gender.

Estimates put the majority of people on this earth in believing in some sort of god to be eighty percent and rising. Discussing the major tenants of organized religion including Christianity, Islam, Judaism, Sikhism, Buddhism and Hinduism, I can conclude that, religiously speaking, most peoples on this earth believe in the virtue of forgiveness as it relates to expectations from God. Therefore, we as a human race support forgiveness over punishment, at least we do in church, temple or wherever we seek religious peace and guidance. As I am writing this paragraph the Washington Post (Barett and Berman 2019) is reporting that the federal government plans to resume capital punishment by executing a number of federal prisoners. Attorney General William Barr ordered the scheduling of five executions for inmates convicted of killing children. Although 21 states have abandoned the death penalty and very few executions are carried out in modern times the Trump administration is pushing back against this trend as they align themselves with the states that still have the death penalty on their books. The government believes that they owe the death penalty to the families of the victims. This leads me to a discussion of basic philosophical attitudes regarding such punishment.

Egalitarianism is a social philosophy which advocates for the removal of inequities among people. But, as the federal government so poignantly argues, our society is bothered and harassed by evil people. This, humans are not equally valued as to their goodness. Simple observations will reveal that people have vast differences in good versus evil manifestations. We have experienced the benefits of wonderful people like Gandhi, Desmond Tutu, Isaac Newton and Shakespeare. And, we have also experienced such hateful aftermaths of evil campaigns by Ted Bundy and Charles Manson, Osama bid Laden and Adolf Hitler. So, the philosophical question remains, do people really have different worth? Do evil people deserve harsher punishment? Realistically, people do not have different worth, we are all crated equal in the eyes of the law. Perhaps we should be willing to judge people on their point of view and we should judge people as they want to be judged. If we are a forgiving society then we should view people as to their happiness, choice, growth, awareness, autonomy and the way they live meaningful lives. Indeed, we are masters of our own universe or authors of our destinies. Regardless of who we are, all of us (in society) share the need to be happy and lead meaningful lives.

Moreover, we all have the capacity to choose a moral life regardless of how smart we are or how we follow our moral compasses. Because we all have the capacity for moral choices we are vulnerable to errors. Thus, we are all equally moral, and subject to making mistakes. And we all equally care about each other and have the capacity to empathize with the less fortunate of the hurting then we share a human point of view. That is, we care about others but we are also prone to make mistakes of judgment in our relationships with others. So, if we accept the notion that we are a forgiving society them we reject the notions of egalitarianism. We can never be equal in our decision making as our choices so widely vary.

In a forgiving society we adopt a human point of view. In fact, a human pint of view is central to understanding forgiveness. We may not know exactly what it is like to be addicted to opiates or alcohol but we can still emphasize with the alcoholic and drug addict. Assuming human value is neutral, and for most human behaviors, we allow social institutions to define moral merits, then an action is to be considered cruel or kind based upon either human condition or social expectations to some degree or another. How then, do we decide to forgive? Is forgiveness more a human condition or a manifestation from a social institution? Do we forgive because the church tells us to, or do we forgive because we are able to emphasize with a poor decision maker? Which is more salient, morality or religion? We wonder, then, if forgiveness is on equal footing, or is there some other influence?

We come to realize, probably through direct experience, that resenting offenders fosters hostility. Most of us have been victims (at some time) and we directly experienced the feelings of ill-will toward the offender. We bring to the equation (to forgive or not to forgive) a scale of forgiveness. One side is unconditional forgiveness and the other punishment.

When we determine a person needs punishment we make judgements based upon the actions of the offender and we try to connect the actions to a measure of wrongfulness. The process of balancing the extent of wrongfulness can also foster resentment. Forgiveness requires respect, compassion, and goodwill, regardless of the act or actions, for society. A moral theory of forgiveness requires all offenders to be forgiven with compassion and respect. Unforgiving an offender keeps the offender from personal growth and everybody should have the ability to grow morally. Everybody has the right to have the opportunity for personal and moral growth leading to a rich and rewarding life. A basic moral principle of justice must include the premise that no person should be forced to sacrifice any benefit afforded to others so others can benefit in significant ways. Today, it seems our legal system lacks the mechanism to keep itself in check. There needs to be a dipstick monitoring levels of official compassion, respect and goodwill. This monitoring system must extend into every aspect of criminal justice including police, courts, corrections, policy makers and the like.

Reform minded advocates for a forgiveness paradigm or a moral theory of justice recognize that all people have the capacity to experience happiness, moral choice, growth and awareness and that we must recognize and identify offenders from this perspective. In order to reform our society needs to be aware of and identify with any people being left out. We need to empathize with the marginalized and the incarcerated. The concept of deserts (or deserved punishment) is a long-standing philosophical tradition which states that at least some criminals deserve punishment. This is a component of morality. At least some of us may conclude that unproductive offenders might deserve punishment more so that a hard working ones. Why do some criminals deserve harsher punishments than others? Is it originality, intellect, skill?

Or, is it the wrongfulness of the act? Or, is it the extent of harm, or how the community was affected? These factors are difficult to sort out morally. A person who commits a crime deserves to be punished. Such a simple concept, but is it? Deserving punishment is very simple but, at the same time, very complex. Our society puts a great deal of confidence in punishment theories but the less explanatory power a concept has the greater the risk of accidental acceptance by moralists. I've always thought that punishment was the easy way out of a problem. Punishment lets society off of the hook when trying to address the real causes of crime; poor standards of living, climate change, mental illness, child abuse, poor schools, bullying, lack of drug treatment, poor interventions strategies, racism and neglectful crime solving strategies. Our society simply incarcerates or executes the problem. Our criminal justice system has become a convenient catch-all for many social problems.

Essentially forgiveness is an attitude and has three basic components (Holmgren 2012) cognitive, affective and motivational. The cognitive component requires the forgiver to be aware of or be cognizant of the issue at hand. The forgiver must be aware of another's suffering and their need for happiness. The affective component is related to the emotional response of the situation. The feeling in the gut, if you will. Here the forgiver feels the pain of another and how much they seek cessation of the emotional pain. Lastly, the motivation component relates to the forgivers' motivation to resolve the situation. The motivated forgiver wants to see the pain abated and happiness return. Motivation is built into forgiveness. If a forgiver is sincere the result will be forgiveness (at some level) notwithstanding counter veining considerations. In other words, a motivated forgiver will do so.

Attitudes toward forgiveness can also be either integrated, conflicted of fragmented. In the integrated scenario, the cognitive, affective and motivational components are fully harmonious with each other. They are inseparable. Morally ideal forgiveness attitudes are always integrated. All of the reasons to forgive are appropriate and clearly understood. There is no room for malady of the spirit. Integrated attitudes are like that of a love from a father toward his children. A father forgives his children without anything in return. No emotional baggage. What happens when one of the components is missing? This may happen when one of the parents suffers from alcoholism. An ailing or addicted parent doesn't necessarily have the capacity to love a child fully. A fragmented attitude is one where one of the components is suppressed. A parent suffering from PTSD, for example, may not have the proper means to intellectualize a situation and respond accordingly. They may avoid feeling any emotions. A fragmented forgiver may believe something to be true but refuses to engage the necessary emotions required to fulfil the task of forgiveness.

Unconditional forgiveness (like a parent forgiving a child) is morally worthy. It is an integrated attitude and can be cultivated within us. Forgiveness can be our response to any wrongdoing if we cultivate this attitude. An attitude of forgiveness, in this case, is a virtue and a morally worthy objective for a fulfilled life. The problem with worthiness, however, can be deceptive. Giving to a charity for the wrong reasons is an example. Our consideration of our human condition is fraught with complexities. So, rhetorically speaking, how do people develop morally appropriate attitudes? What if a person holds onto deep resentment? Resentment can be an expected response to wrongs committed against us. Accordingly, we feel guilty when we wrong somebody, indignation when we hear about somebody else being wronged, and resentment when we are wronged. The cognitive component recognizes that an individual has harmed us. Somebody has done something morally inappropriate toward us. The affective component eludes a moral response, anger probably. And the motivational component seeks moral order be restored. But resentment is pervasive. However, resentment does necessarily have to include vindictiveness or retaliation. A domestic violence victim, for example, will simply want the abuse to go away. Also, a victim may withdrawal goodwill until the wrong has been righted. The extent of the withdrawal of goodwill depends upon the gravity of the offense.

Forgiveness, on the other hand, requires a change of heart. Resentment is overcome with replaced with a positive attitude. Forgiveness becomes a corrective attitude that replaces resentment as it's no longer deemed necessary. Genuine forgiveness must be articulated as a clear change of attitude. A change of heart must coincide with a change in judgement toward the offender and or the event. A victim's viewpoint must be significantly revised in order for the forgiveness to be genuine. When a wronged person forgives, the offender is recognized as being wrong and that they were responsible for the misdeeds. The person that forgives holds salient beliefs beyond that of the offender. The cognitive approach views the offender as having the potential of being happy or miserable but really wants to be happy. The forgiver knows the probability of the offender being rather week and possibly being confused and vulnerable. We also know that the offender is a valuable human being and has at least some status of their own. On the other hand, the affective component consists of feeling compassion and kindness to the wrongdoer. A victim may find new joy in a forgiving relationship.

A motivational component sees a desire for good things to happen for the offender. Apathy for an offender is not a virtue, a desire for goodwill and happiness is.

Holmgren (2012) puts together some ways to differentiate between three necessary components of forgiveness, cognitive, affective and motivational. Holmgren developed ways for the scholar of forgiveness to start thinking about the depth and breadth of the issues contained in the forgiveness decision. Along these lines Enright and Coyle (1998) further dissect the forgiveness process and present this as a moral development model. The model contains stages of reasoning. Forgiveness occurs when the victim changes their viewpoint toward the offender and begins to see the wrongdoer with compassion. Forgiveness requires strength, courage and mercy. Genuine forgiveness is always voluntary and is genuinely transformative. The victim is transformed and hopefully so is the wrongdoer, even though it is not a necessary condition for forgiveness to take place. The propensity for a victim to forgive depends upon a number of variables including, age, the present and intensity of an apology, the probability of future harm, and proximity of the wrongdoer, severity of the offense and the attitude of the offender. Accordingly, Enright and Cole (1998) were able to scale the propensity of forgiveness on a scale from always forgive to never forgive. Think about this. Haven't we been wronged over our lifetimes and we've found way to forgive but not each case is equally valued? But most people, they found, followed a path starting with their propensity to forgive and the cancellation of their consequences while considering the intent, proximity and apologies of the wrongdoer.

Forgiveness Can Happen Through Any Number of Channels.

A victim can simply stop thinking about the event (cognitive) they can stop feeling angry (affective) they can seek nothing (behavioral) or they can let God handle it (take the spiritual route). Regardless of how one decides to forgive (the research shows that) forgiveness generally increases mental health and improves relationships. Failing to forgive, on the contrary, can evoke pathological problems, including revenge fantasies and serious blaming, or, if the victim is more withdrawn poor recovery from bereavement and can affect overall physical and emotional health. Many incidents of emotional transgressions begin with the wrongdoer's repentance. Forgiveness can follow a sincere repent. The emotional benefits of accepting a wrongdoer's repentance and followed with true forgiveness can be very personal and can lead to spiritual peace. The problem is, in public, life transgressions are hard to keep secret and forcing repentance and forgiveness into an open forum can inhibit the beneficial aspects of a private interchange and transgression. If for whatever reason, forgiveness must occur in a public place, and the interpersonal zone has evaporated, what are the costs associated with accepting the repentance and forgiving? The spiritual benefits may be compromised. Complicating these scenarios and concepts are the fact that both the victim and the wrongdoer can actually be in both roles simultaneously. When family members, siblings, married couples, or folks that put themselves in a volatile situation the role of victim and offender can be blurred. Like in an automobile accident, for example, both drivers can sometimes contribute to the crash.

Most forgiveness takes place implicitly. The victim simply forgives. There is nothing else said. Repentance can also be implicit but the wrongdoer may respond by giving candy, flowers, gifts or other nice behavior without asking for forgiveness.

People can also agree to get along and bury the episode. They go about with their lives without bringing the incident up. People agree to reconciliation by agreeing to make the feelings go away. Of course there are all sorts of combinations of repentance and forgiveness depending upon the degree of repentance. A low degree of repentance will result in a low level of forgiveness. The victim may feel better if they know the wrongdoer feels guilty. Can we agree that a bit of expressed guilt can start the forgiveness process? At the very least, expressions of forgiveness ought to de-escalate the objectionable behavior. Even implicit forgiveness reduces guilt and helps to restore confidence and harmony. We really want harmony don't we? Forgiveness also takes away the role of the victim. It takes away the weakness and may mitigate the degree of cruelty that exists between the wrongdoer and the victim.

When we contemplate shared humanity and we see others as human the defining operative here may be forgiveness. Consider religious groups. A closed religious group, like a cult, is unforgiving and an open religious group is openly forgiving of others and their capacity to see others in the context of their humanity is the key to their identity. Forgiveness may offer humanity a way to deal with confusion and cultural migration or change. The more forgiving a group is the easier they come to reduce resentment and hostility. When others do evil things our morality is tested. Do we respond to evil via strict moral codes (clear rules of right and wrong) or do we respond emotionally and lean toward a humanistic code of forgiveness?

Morton and Postmes (2010) studied groups and their shared humanity. Importantly, they found that problematic histories fuel intergroup conflict and further reluctance to seek forgiveness. Thus, they find that arriving at a shared understanding of history is a critical part of reconciling between groups.

Defensiveness is pervasive between groups with a shared conflicted history and the goal is to find ways for groups to move beyond their pasts into a more positive future. How groups see themselves in relation to other groups shapes their collective attitude. Groups can either be a victimized group or a perpetrator group. How groups see themselves can shape their perceptions of humanity. What humans do (or don't do) shapes their humanity. Morton and Postmes further describe theses in-groups and out-groups in terms of their shared humanity. Their first hypothesis is shared humanity can result in forgiveness. Or, the more groups forgive others the more they are seen as humanistic. The second hypothesis is that group identity can favor in-group over out-group. The researchers believe that we should strive to move people away from single common identities. Groups should strive to find a common (shared) identity that extends favorability. We need to find ways to see others in terms of their humanity. People tend to share humanity within their own in-group. We need to beware that we don't perceive others as lees human. This can justify immoral behavior. In-groups, over time, can become more self-inclusive and definitions of groups can become more abstract. If definitions of groups become abstract the in-group members can come up with ways to ill define others in a us versus them fashion. Or, even worse, a more obscene way. In-groups tend to lesson responsibility for their feelings toward others as they find ways to ease their guilt by seeing themselves as more human that than the out-group. In-group members see themselves as the only human group and this diminishes responsibility for the ill will toward the out-group. But, if in-groups seek to engage the out-groups some feelings of humanizing will take place. Self- humanizing in-groups may seek moral disengagement.

Shared humanity can deflect notions of guilt and should promote forgiveness and reconciliation. But, perpetrator groups may hide behind their humanity and deflect responsibility for their wrongfulness. Thus, dehumanization of outgroups can be a mechanism of moral disengagement. Out-groups, when dehumanized feel rightfully justified regarding their illegitimacy. We are only human not to be blamed. So, group identify as a victim of a perpetrator can foster long standing ill will between groups. Again, shared humanity should promote reconciliation and forgiveness. In-groups and out-groups can feel severely discriminated against. Some groups have been victims of war or other purposeful acts committed against a group. This is not a simple fix. We should strive for forgiveness as we mature as a culture.

Holmgren points out that regardless of the type of victim or intensity of resentment nobody can forgive somebody else on behalf of somebody else. Forgiveness requires an internal change of heart. As we mature our goal is to cultivate attitudes that we find morally worthy. But, by trial and error, we learn through the maturing process witch behavior yields moral rewards. In the end we choose to forgive because we see the offender as a person who warrants respect, has compassion as the result of the forgiveness as well as a sense of goodwill. When we forgive we don't necessarily forget the incident. We no longer remember the incident with vindictiveness. We learn to regard the incident with objectiveness. When we forgive we make peace with the past and no longer fell the need to concern ourselves with it.

Genuine forgiveness can be difficult. It requires letting go of anger and recovering lost dignity. Reconciliation requires compassion, understanding and trust.

Reconciliation requires acceptance of the wrongdoer, good feelings too, and a general sense of harmony between the victim and perpetrator. Sometimes, a relationship must end in order to restore harmony. Many people believe that restoration must include at least some punishment and restitution. These acts, it is believed, will serve to prevent future wrongdoing. But, many also believe that punishment and restitution strategies are incompatible with the true spirit of forgiveness. Forgives is more that hearing the words, "I'm sorry or I forgive you." These words may indeed be true but the utterance of these words is no guarantee of absence of bitterness. Forgiveness requires some degree of behavioral consequences.

Huxley, in his quest to find the ultimate truth, concluded that through God people learn to be calm and happy. They practice traits of goodness, have wisdom and mercy. Within groups they feel love toward others in their group, and hopefully they also feel and seek to feel love toward out-groups. A troubled, godless mind, on the other hand results in a person feeling upset and anxious. They are filled with fear, hate, envy and anger toward others. In Huxley's Perennial Philosophy he seeks to find the highest common factor in all existing theories. He seeks one divine reality. In criminology I wonder who set the stage for our reality when it comes to dealing with crime and criminals. Who has figured this out? What really matters in the field of criminology? What are the best (agreed upon) practices? Our criminological truth answers the question of what really matters. What is success in criminology? And what is a failure? And how we treat each other needs to be connected to our divine truth. The truth is we rely upon the criminal code (the written law) to set the behavioral line in the sand, defining the concepts of right and wrong. The law prescribes punishment. The truth of the law is that it assumes sane people make calculated decisions.

Our legal codes assume people do not commit wrongs because they fear punishment. The legal codes also recognizes the fact that actions have varying degrees of malice, strange motives and the possibility of accidental injury. The balancing of these concepts often times relies on direction as decision makers decide who is to be processed and who is not. The criminal justice system is also perplexed with the issues of unreported crime otherwise known as the dark figure of crime. Many wrongdoers are never really discovered.

The truth is our law is not an end all for all social problems. The law is a social construct and is supposed to deter crime. But, most crime goes unreported and most of the crimes that are reported go unsolved. The truth is about crime is that crime is normal and sometimes even desirable. Crime is often caused by social conditions like political struggles, and rapid change that the criminal justice system cannot control. Moreover, people are willful and will choses to commit crime or refrain for it too. Crime is often rooted in emotions like greed and is learned as a response many times within families. We also know that serious street crimes are rooted deep within the lower class. So, any new philosophy of criminality must address virtuous behavior. It's not enough to lay out the wrongs as a baseline for a theory. Instead we need to figure out language to replace hatred with love, parlay the benefits of resignation to our culture, teach obedience to the nature of things and learn to quell our desires into a state of desirelessness.

Chapter 3

Psychology and Forgiveness

Gull and Rana (2013) studied a sample of professional people seeking to find the respondents' level of awareness as to the benefits of forgiveness. They found that respondents knew the importance of forgiveness as an issue affecting their quality of life. The research sought to discover if feelings of forgiveness attributed toward a better quality of life manifested through measurable levels of happiness, positivity, relaxation, contentment and spiritual development. When the researchers controlled for gender, they found that women reported a more satisfied life, with higher levels of wellbeing and tolerance. When a victim forgives the wrongdoer their feelings of resentment and anger are abated by feelings of goodwill. Forgiveness frees the victim from negative attachments to the offender. Moreover, forgiveness is a psychological process where feelings of resentment, anger or indignation cease to exist against the wrongdoer. The demands for restitution or punishment are diminished and reconciliation can lead to a happier emotional life.

Forgiveness can also lead to improved physical lives as well. An improved emotional life leads to a better physical life. A forgiving person lives a life of improved relationships. We know that relationships become more stable and mutually supportive of others. Proponents of positive emotional psychology highlight the noted higher levels of emotional intelligence that include factors such as humility, humor, hope, love, empathy, altruism, positive responses to a loss, creativity, morality, spirituality and well-being. In other words forgiving people are quantifiable happier than non-forgiving people. The aforementioned study also found that forgiving people had better relationships with other people in their social networks and a higher rate of disease prevention.

On the other hand, unforgiving people who engage in unforgiving imagery tend to rehearse hurtful memories and hold grudges. These negative emotions can cause higher EMG results, skin conductance, higher heart rates, and raised base-line blood pressure. Also, hostility toward others is an independent risk factor for coronary heart disease and premature death. Gull and Rana concluded that people who live a life with a manifestation of forgiveness receive nine marked benefits and positive effects on their personality. The most reported feeling was a life of happiness and a life including positive feelings. They also indicate that people who talk about their forgiveness experience with others greatly enhance their social well-being.

The psychological benefits of forgiveness include the benefits realized in restored relationships. Forgiveness also reduces guilt and increases confidence in relationships. Forgiveness helps to erase the roles of the victim and the wrongdoer and forgiveness cancels the debt while it removes weakness from the parties involved. Moreover, it eliminates the feelings associated with being a victim and forgiveness helps to level the playing field. Both victim and offender can be equal and each can see each other as a person of value. And as previously indicated, forgiveness greatly increases health benefits.

Getting prepared to forgive can be a daunting emotional process. Many times victims are wrought with anger, bitterness and defensiveness. Simultaneously, the wrongdoer may be reticent to offer repentance because the victim will expect a combination of confession, apology and restitution. A perpetrator may fear such a confession or disagree with the level of wrongdoing they committed, further complicating the process. A confession may also open the door to unknown incidents or suspicions of such incidents.

Criminals are very likely to downplay their actions as impulsive uncontrollable or somehow justifiable due to some perceived mitigating circumstance. Perpetrators often try to mitigate their role in a crime by downplaying the role they took in it. Criminals want to believe that what they did was actually less harmful, les malicious and more justifiable then portrayed. This difference between the victim's viewpoint and the perpetrator's perception of the incident is known as a magnitude gap. Magnitude gaps are self-serving distortions of the truth and perpetrators can also frequently see themselves as victims. Aggressive male criminals see slights to their manhood as affronts to their self-esteem, where others do not. Perpetrators tend to become defensive when confronted, especially by an angry victim. Or, in a marriage, perhaps, both husband and wife are equally culpable in a transgression.

Wrongdoers may not want to accept the guilt associated with repentance. They see the guilt laid onto them by the victims as being excessive. And a criminal will certainly avoid any form of confession if he/she feels a slightest chance a criminal charge can be avoided. Our criminal justice system carries with it the presumption of innocence but the gate-keepers in the criminal justice system like spontaneous confessions. They seem more genuine and more positive toward the victim. But not confessing, which is expected in most incidents, may keep the police from discovering the transgression. Of course a confession or admission of guilt may result in the loss of freedom for the accused. Trying to remain absolutely silent in the face of a jail stint seems to be the best strategy, at least in the short run. Plus, if they confess, and the go to jail, they will most likely never confess again. We can imagine that for an alcoholic to admit to be an alcoholic is very difficult as they'll have to stop drinking.

Wrongdoers may also be reluctant to confess because they will be ashamed. Guilt is associated with a specific action but shame is a perception that affects the entire self. Shame is a self-loathing emotion. A shameful person wants to hide. Shameful people may also become aggressive, angry, blameful, and suspicious. They can be suicidal and revengeful. Guilt may press a person toward confession but shame results in hiding or blaming. Shame can be especially poignant when immoral acts are involved. It is hard to confess to an immoral act. Shame may also be morally downgrading. Shame can effectively change to superiority dynamics in a relationship further compounding any chances of a resolution. A shameful person may not be able to maintain their position of superiority which is very important to many people in a relationship. A shameful perpetrator may feel vulnerable or afraid of the victim. This is especially true if the victim is unaware of the immoral act perpetrated by their partner.

Forgiveness involves cancelling the debt. Intrapsychic forgiveness requires the mental cancellation of a debt. By giving up on the perpetrator the victim relinquishes something while realizing they will, in the future, never receive anything in return. When a victim forgives an interpersonal debt they are allowing themselves to be victimized again. Thus, forgiving in this fashion can be risky especially is the wrongdoer is not repentant. This happens in close relationships. Incidents can be sever, repeated, forgiven, and repeated again and these actions can be quite intentional and filled with malice. The cyclical nature of this type of forgiveness and non-forgiveness in close relationships may be due to the fact that the forgiveness is mostly done implicitly, rather than explicitly. Victims chooses to forgive in non- communitive or non-confrontational means. This is done to ease the friction due to the forgiveness moment. In these cases the forgiveness gets lost in the translation. The victim and the wrongdoer have grown to mistrust each other. The repeated transgressions have not served to build trust. Therefore, the victim has a generalized fear of trusting the wrongdoer. This is especially true in domestic violence situations where repeated transgressions are common.

Others may fear forgiving because it may make the victim appear weak, vulnerable or timid to others. They would rather safe face and not back down. This vulnerability and fear can cause a victim to become humiliated and vengeful. When we think about this, forgiveness returns power to the victim. In a forgiveness paradigm, it may be that justice is not served. There will be no eye for an eye. To forgive might be morally regretful and forgiving creates a loss to the victim. The power to induce guilt or demand an apology can be powerful. Plus, acting the victim can have substantial rewards. Holding a grudge gives power to the victim in a relationship. They can easily justify anger and indignation and they can solicit support from others. Before a victim forgives they should know that the right to claim justice is waived. Before this can happen they may need to address their vulnerability and feelings about safety. And there are no guarantees that the actor will not do the same thing to you again.

Asking for forgiveness has its own set of obstacles and it can be hard on the ego. The wrongdoer will have to give up their self-image. The wrongdoer will have to give up claims to be moral. After all, a confession is telling all about a person and the power in the relationship will be altered in favor of the victim. Telling somebody that you are wrong means they'll be forced to accept a negative moral evaluation of themselves. Humiliation may result after a wrongdoer openly admits to their transgressions.

When people confess they do so at considerable risk to their self-interest. Offenders fear shame and further punishment. Again, offenders believe that their deeds are not as serious as the victim lays them out to be.

We ought to encourage forgiveness. We, are all fallible and do bad things, just like the next guy. Each of us is equally susceptible to temptations and vulnerable to bad acts. If you want to restore your relationship with the offender then you'll have to forgive them. If not, your ability to have friends is at risk. Forgiving will facilitate the victim getting on with their lives. Maybe this is selfish, but forgiving is a rationale choice and it releases one from the perpetrator. Plus, forgiving is the right thing to do.

The forgiveness process may be evolutionary as a brain function. Encephalization is a type of neuro-evolutionary process that considers the evolution of the brain. Science knows that frontal lobe activity is associated with a sense of self. An injury to oneself, for example, provides a perception of self. The brain, over time, learns to discern between behaviors that are injurious and beneficial to self. And the brain records such discernment as a memory, especially that memory of an injurious person. The frontal lobe has the capacity for abstraction and reification or the ability to generate classes of object. The frontal lobe can distinguish between things. A self-reflection evolves. The ability for the brain to evoke emotions is a function of the inferior parietal lobule on the dominate side. As our perceptions of ego expand we tend to emerge with an exaggerated sense of ourselves, and at the same time, a lesser view of others. We have evolved to maintain the perseverance of self beyond all other things.

We, therefore, perceive emotions to be product of our own selves and not others. We have evolved to be a people with a greater perception of self along with all things associated with ourselves.

Conspecific congruence is a perceived nonhierarchical relationship between individuals and other members of the group. This is a powerful psychological force that create or limits the structure of relationships and roles within social groups. We see that, generally speaking, pro- aristocratic elements conflict with proto-democratic psychological elements creating pressure within all social groups. Conspecific congruence helps create a balance within the social group so all members understand their roles and relationships with all other in the social group. Conspecific congruence occurs when all members behave to maintain a social balance. Belonging to a group provides us with the vehicle to form "us" verses "them" definitions. A change in the congruence of an injurious attack will result in revenge to restore the congruence. Because humans have a self-world congruence we can relate ourselves within the spectrum of all others in the world. The sense of belonging to a group is a powerful motivation to stay aligned with that group.

Forgiveness as being evolutionary is possible as we see that justice has always been included as a necessary condition for preservation of societies and cultures. An eye for an eye is the most primitive manifestation of justice and a clear manifestation of personal revenge. True revenge is an elaboration of the self-preservation motif. True revenge is an attempt to equalize congruency between conspecifics. When a member gets injured there is a strong there is (and was) a strong impulse to return the hurt and address the imbalance.

Disequilibrium is caused by perceived hurt or injury generating a desire in the injured party's mind to restore balance by getting revenge. If forgiveness requires the foreswearing of resentment, then, at a more primitive time, forgiveness foreswears revenge. Either way the objective is to out the memory of the injury. The neuropsychology of forgiveness relates to the substrates of injury perception in revenge. In other words, the response to injury is adaptive as one seeks advantages of conspecific congruence. Forgiveness requires a person to give up on redressing a wrong in the traditional way. Submission as an example, as we see in the animal world.

Why would forgiveness in human societies evolve? What are the adaptive strategies? If we continue to see ourselves as exalted, then our perpetrator is also exalted. Unless we forgive the perpetrator we will never realize equilibrium. Instead, we will experience social chaos. Forgiveness can be the key to eliminate hostility. Forgiveness, then, can also generate empathy and warmth for the victim. Forgiveness can have remarkably profound consequences and people experiencing or seeing honest forgiveness can actually realize a religious experience. Generally speaking, an empathetic response to a forgiving person may be a primary evolved component to forgiveness. Here forgiveness is profitable for social groups as it fosters evolutionary change. Revenge is based upon over-emphasized perceptions of self-importance. Indeed, the benefits of forgiveness far outweigh the benefits of revenge. Over time forgiveness may actually serve to add cohesion to social groups. Forgiveness enhances social adhesion by discouraging violations of other's rights. Forgiveness allows for better modulation and control of revenge. One day forgiveness could become an obligation.

Grudge Theory

Forgiveness is a significant pro-social phenomenon. It benefits social life by allowing relationships to heal. Forgiveness happens within the heart and mind of the victim. This emotionally-charged decision has two paths, one to forgive the other not forgive. To not forgive suggests that the victim will hold a grudge and adhere to negative feelings (Baumeister, Exline and Sommer 1998). Forgiveness brings negative feeling to an end. Holding a grudge and sustaining anger over time is unpleasant, stressful and can be extremely unhealthy. When we consider the value of the victim's peace of mind, forgiveness may be the only answer, regardless of the relationship between the wronged and the wrongdoer. The two dimensions of forgiveness are inner and interpersonal. The inner dimension refers to the emotional and cognitive state of the victim. The interpersonal dimension involves the ongoing relationship where the forgiveness outcome does or does not take place. People who have suffered at the hand of another, try to make sense of their situations and reduce the negative aspects of their trauma. They realize, at some level, that forgiveness is the only real option to return the victim to a state of normalcy, or a state of forgiveness. Grudge theory and forgiveness theory mirror each other. They are opposites each other. The relationship between these opposites can become blurry. Forgiveness may mean one thing to the victim and yet, something else to the wrongdoer. This blurriness can cause serious misunderstandings.

A transgression is an act or action that goes against an expected norm. It can be crime or an offense. If there were never any transgressions there would never be the need for forgiveness. A theory of evil explains the perceptions of transgressions, their consequences and the role of forgiveness.

Forgiveness brings to an end the detrimental effects of a transgression. We seek to bring the situation back to normal. The "back to normal" situation requires a rejection of the role of victim. A wronged will say, "I am no longer a victim." The alternative is to hold grudge. Some perpetrators want to be forgiven. They genuinely feel remorse. They are sorry for what they did. Many others are unrepentant. They do not admit anything, or take responsibility for their transgressions or acknowledge any wrongdoing. The manners and attitudes of the wrongdoer mater to the victim. The perpetrator plays a significant role in the motivation for the victim to forgive. Does the perpetrator feel guilty over the transgression? Guilt may be the motivator for the wrongdoer to apologize for the transgression. If there is an absence of guilt, there is no acknowledgement of the transgression. Forgiveness offers the cancellation of the guilt.

Thus, there is a cost/benefit process here for the victim. For the forgiver there is a cost. The victim must give up something. The wronged will have to agree to be poorer in some way. Consider the scenario where the wronged gives up every debt ever owed to them. Once, they forgive they give up any future right to extract concessions, compromises or compliance. A non-forgiving person is a grudge holder. People have valid reasons for not forgiving. We all hold back on certain aspects of this. It is human nature to protect ourselves form future harm, plus, wrongdoers and victim have differing points of view. Victims may exaggerate their experience and perpetrators may downplay their role in the event. Victims may see their perpetrator's actions as ongoing bad behavior, inexcusable, immoral and gratuitous, and possibly cruel. Perpetrators, on the other hand, tend to blame others s they strive to justify their behavior, make sense of their wrongdoings and build a case for legitimacy. These differences can complicate the tasks of forgiveness.

The average perpetrator is very willing to let bygones be bygones. Or, the perpetrator may be clues as to the costs of their malfeasance. The victim always has to give something up. The wrongdoer, not so. The debt can be hard to balance. When evil occurs there exists a magnitude gap. The victim loses more than the perpetrator gains. Thus, vendettas can arise as there appears to be no way to balance the ledger. Conventional wisdom leads us to believe that victims tell the truth and victims lie. But the reality is that both distort the circumstances of the event. The wrongdoers leave out the worst parts and the victims omit mitigating factors favoring the perpetrator. Balancing the debt can be difficult to negotiate because the negotiation process is between two people with opposite viewpoints. Forgiveness is a social action. It occurs between two people with the objective of restoring parties to a previous state. Forgiveness happens inside of people and it happens between people. Thus is has two dimensions. To forgive somebody means to forget feelings of anger and resentment over the transactions. The "act" of forgiveness happens in the mind of the victim (intrapsychic). So, balancing the ledger can happen.

Hollow forgiveness can occur when a victim orally expresses forgiveness but this interpersonal act is happening without the intrapsychic state. The victim may find it palpable to say the words, "I forgive you" but still can't reconcile the feelings associated with the magnitude gap. The expressions of forgiveness are present but inside the victim the issue remains unresolved. The hurt remains but the wrongdoer is done with it. The wrongdoer assumes forgiveness. After all, the wronged said I forgive you. In order for the act of forgiveness to be genuine the victim has to surrender their high moral ground. Being a victim comes with a feeling of superiority over the wrongdoer. They feel entitled to special treatment.

A forgiving victim gives up the moral high ground and the superiority. Once they forgive, there is no reversal. A forgiver cannot go back on his word.

Forgiveness also contains a time dimension. The process of attaining full forgiveness, opposed to a one-sided forgiveness, takes time. In fact, it can take a long time. Sometimes to forgiveness can begin silently. The victim, in these cases, stops feeling resentful and angry but nothing is ever conveyed to the wrongdoer. This "silent forgiveness "happens when the victim allows the wrongdoer to continue to feel guilty. The victim has removed the negativity of the grudge by letting it go. The negative effects are eliminated. It also avoids any concessions. The silent forgiveness can be problematic in a relationship. It can create an emotional imbalance if one party forgives in silence. The transgressor's guilt remains further adding tension to the relationship. If the transgressor is forgiven totally then the ill feelings and guilt are released. No forgiveness is holding a grudge. The victim chooses not to forgive. The victim may hold out for some monetary or emotional reward.

An unforgiveable wrong may occur in a marriage, for example. In this case a victim might decide to stay in the marriage and wait for appropriate rewards that lead up to total forgiveness. The victim can continue to claim a moral high ground and be righteously indignant. By prolonging the total forgiveness the spouse may desire to teach the other a lesson. The lingering memory of the transgression always remains. The unforgiving spouse can retain the role of victim indefinitely. They will maintain the vantage point. One can opt to continue to suffer. Maybe it is appropriate is a spouse has been murdered, for example. Your sense of loss will continue forever. But, as long as the victim stays on the unforgiving course in this journey, the transgression continues.

Sometimes reconciliation is not possible. Some actions are unforgivable. But, how long can we suffer? Forgiving can cause loss of face. Others may criticize or see the forgiver as week or foolish. Wounded pride may be the catalyst for change. But, what about revenge? A blow to one's pride is a fore step toward seeking revenge. An injured pride is a powerful stimulus to seek paybacks. Indeed, a blow to self-esteem (overt disrespect, in front of witnesses) can lead to interpersonal violence. Many will choose to hold onto a grudge that to surrender their pride. Plus, some acts are utterly reprehensible and if we forgive these acts it may seem to others that we are condoning them. However, grudge holding has costs. It perpetrates further suffering and distress. Holding a grudge can cause further unhappiness and add fuel to the fire of an angry person. A grudge holder may also suffer from the effects of emotional corrosiveness, unpleasantness and unhealthiness. The grudge holder may create a life for themselves that is a cycle of unhappy living as they repeatedly repeat overt negative emotions. Holding grudges will hamper further relationships and even professional opportunities. A grudge-holding victim will breed passivity and continued failure. Victims in a grudge holding role turn themselves into people who are more passive, slower and more willing to give up when faced with difficulties. A grudge can kill a relationship. Forgiveness is an effort to repair a relationship damaged by a transgression but holding onto a grudge can lead to the termination of the relationship. If the transgressor makes amends and promises never to repeat the activity them there is no reasonable incentive to hold a grudge. Our individual and collective futures depends upon the degree to which we are willing to forgive.

When we forgive we replace resentment with an attitude of respect, compassion and goodwill for to offender.

Conversely, when we do wrong we can be beset with feelings of guilt and self-condemnation. We can become self-condemning when we become aware that we have hurt somebody. We acknowledge their suffering and pain. When we self-condemn we feel shame and moral anger. Or self-assessment can result in feelings of remorse, anguish, despair and self-doubt. If all goes as expected a desire emerges to effect change. Sometimes to change comes as the result of the wrongdoer taking on the feelings of the victim. The urge to repent and do penance can result as the wrongdoer experiences this pain. In the extreme case, suicide will result.

Self-forgiveness, on the other hand, requires the personal recognition that we did, in fact, do something wrong. Self-forgiveness has components of self-worth, capacity for personal growth, the development of purposeful choice and awareness. Plus, self-respect and acceptance of one's role in the malfeasance and resolve. A self-forgiving person will regret what happened but not hold themselves in contempt. They will not punish themselves and live their lives in a peaceful, meaningful and constructive manner. Self-forgiveness begins with the wrongdoer addressing the problem with self-respect. They admit that they did something wrong and take full responsibility for the wrong. They fully recognize the status of the victim. They must learn to see the victim in human terms including all of their feeling and vulnerabilities. The wrongdoer must recognize the feelings and manifestations arising from the event. This is done in order to connect the offender to what they have done. The offender needs to address the behavior patterns that led them to behave in the way they did. They must address their character flaws that lead them to the wrongdoing. Finally, they need to make amends. There may be fines or restitution to pay. The wrongdoer must acknowledge the pain and suffering they caused and take full responsibility for them as well as take the responsibility for correcting their attitudes as they make amends.

After a serious moral failure, a person must regain their bearings and accept their shortcomings. They need to forgive themselves. A transgressor who refuses to forgive them self is on a path of self-destruction. Some may argue that if the focus is on the transgressor then the victim will be ignored. But, what if the victim refuses to cooperate or the victim has moved away or died? If the victim refuses to forgive or pardon the wrongdoer then the offender must constitute an approximation of forgiveness. After all, any attempts to approach the victim might make matters worse or may be seen as disrespectful. But the offender is obligated to correct the wrong. The wrongdoer may not be able to replace what has been lost or they might not be physically able to make reparations. So, the offender must still try to fulfill their obligations to the victim or do what they can. Once the wrongdoer has done all they can do to fill the obligations they are done. The offender must renounce what they did and make every effort to make amends to the victim, but at the same time, they must not renounce themselves. The offender needs to recognize their intrinsic value.

What if the victim refuses to forgive? Do victims always have the exclusive right to forgive? Goodwill can only come about if the offender remains a valuable human being who warrant respect, compassion and goodwill. The victim can be in the position to act as a catalyst as the offender moves toward self-forgiveness. In any event, the offender must recognize their self-worth and forgive themselves regardless of the position of the victim. In serious cases the offender must fully acknowledge the extent of their harm and do everything possible to correct it.

The goal here is to eliminate any residual negative attitudes either way between the victim and the offender. An attitude of self-condemnation does not further the case for forgiveness. It is less than respectful. Proper and correct respectful attitudes toward the victim should be focused squarely on the victim. One cannot hide self-deficiencies by over-respecting the victim. Nevertheless, self-forgiveness may hold the key for real positive change. Once the offender has worked through their wrongs a change will be cultivated from within resulting in a true respect for morality.

It is unlikely that one will hold onto a sense of morality while simultaneously holding onto an attitude of self-condemnation. Developing a true sense of respect and compassion for the victim will serve to motivate an offender to avoid hurting other sin the future. As one addresses the defects in character that led one to do the wrongs that they did an understanding will come to pass. Only self-respect will allow this journey to be completed. Self-respect will lead to a life with moral integrity. It seems an offender's character traits can be eradicated with compassion, respect and goodwill. People who view themselves with self-condemnation will view others similarly. The wrongful act is the event that gets trapped in the offender's mind. They keep viewing themselves with contemp. If we are ever to respect ourselves as moral agents then we must be responsible for our past actions. But it doesn't have to result in self-condemnation. After all, self-respect is a self-evaluative process. How do we decide what is right behavior? Improvement oriented self-assessment is of critical importance as we try to be normative moral exemplars. None of us is a saint so we must learn to appropriately adapt to shifting circumstances.

Restorative justice may require punishment. Some might deserve to be punished. But morality sometimes calls for harsh responses. We find ourselves puzzled as how to handle future wrongs but we also know that self-reproach helps us define who we are. When we are able to replace attitudes of self-condemnation with self-forgiveness we realize we don't have to behave that way in the future. To over dwell on the past will cause us to develop attitudes of self-contempt. When we do something wrong hopefully we do our best to address it. And we care about the suffering inflicted on others. We should put our efforts into correcting the wrongs and making contributions to others.

Lander (2016) believes in the strength of forgiveness therapy in the social work field. His study points out that when un-forgiveness persists negative feelings, along with psychological, cognitive and behavioral corollaries, related to a transgression remain salient. Mental health and quality of life for the victim can result. The benefits of forgiveness in his field are considered to be healthy, courageous and humanizing. Moreover, forgiveness is related to a positive outlook, self-acceptance, environmental mastery and improved physical health.

Forgiveness is the transformative act of a person unfairly and profoundly hurt. The negative feelings associated with the hurt including anger, hate and hostility are lessened when forgiveness is realized. Forgiveness also significantly reduces the need for a victim to seek revenge. We should agree that the explicit goal of forgiveness in therapy as worthwhile and beneficial. In social work clients are often exposed to different perspectives and alternative ways of seeing things. The therapist tries to get the victim to take responsibility and enhance their life's situation. Forgiveness therapy offers the client an option for resolving a significant past injury.

Talking about forgiveness helps the therapist find the deep seated emotions of the maltreatment. Then the negative feelings including disappointment, shame and anger can be addressed. Forgiveness helps the therapist to establish and maintain a healthy relationship. The use of forgiveness in social work can be a promising therapeutic method in many aspects of practice where interpersonal and self- injury is being addressed.

Some of the forgiveness therapy models suggest a rather purposeful number of steps can be employed to foster forgiveness in a victim. Enright and Coyle (1998) posit a five step process beginning with uncovering. Uncovering is followed by decision making, then work and finally deepening. Martin and Thoresen (1997) suggest a six phase therapeutic forgiveness process. Their model starts with exposure. Then follow with acknowledgement, forgiveness, healing, approaching the wrongdoer and finally reducing the future hurts. These steps suggest that forgiveness models can be repeated, monitored and taught to students of forgiveness therapy. Forgiveness therapy can employ vestiges of cognitive therapy where victims become more aware of their feelings and how their mind is processing the victimization. Anger and hostility small group therapy sessions also have utility. As does self-efficacy therapy where therapists apply humanity and compassion to others in a loving fashion. As we already discussed forgiveness therapy can bring joy and enthusiasm to a person's life. Other therapeutic models begin with trying to elicit the victim's awareness and acceptance of their emotions. These emotions may include anger, sadness, and maybe even loss. Next, the therapist urges the client to let these feelings go. They need to be released as they learn that there is little they can do about resolving them. Next, the therapist wants to shift the view of the offender from blame and seeking punishment to something more positive.

The process seeks to actively change the viewpoint of the offender to one of empathy and understanding. Eventually, a new narrative of the self and the wrongdoer will emerge. The victims shift to a new light. They now see the offender in a new perspective. In this manner, forgiveness is a process of therapeutically urged change. The necessary components for this process include awareness of emotions, letting go of unmet needs, a shift of viewpoint of the offender, empathy for the wrongdoer and finally a construction of a new narrative. By letting go, victims can be released of all efforts trying to make others try and understand their feeling. They can stop trying to get the offender to take responsibility. By letting go empathy can emerge. Forgiving people see their offenders in a new light. These new views can include both positive and negative images.

There are a couple of ways to build models of forgiveness. Therapists can employ task analysis or models that look for resolution of unfinished business. The task analysis models seek to first, define the problem, then discover how the problem might be resolved. Then, you look for ways to develop problem solving techniques and finally, go out and employ the model with help from somebody with the skill to offer follow-up and feedback. The resolution of unfinished business model looks to resolve lingering unresolved feelings toward the offender. This may help to ease frustration resulting from separation, abandonment or abuse. The process begins with a self-evaluation, followed with a self-assertion where others are held accountable. The idea is to identify the components of the conflict and resolve lingering feelings.

The Pyramid Model put forth by Worthington (1998) puts steps in place that a therapist and the client can process the forgiveness.

The steps start with recalling the hurt, followed with empathizing with the person who hurt you. The third step is altruistic gift and step four is the commitment to forgive. When we are conditioned not to feel hurt we may freeze or become over-stressed causing a withdrawal, fight or submission. The first step, then, recalling the hurt, considers the unforgiving person and recognizes their pain, their tension, stress, withdrawal, anger, and retaliatory responses. Here they work on issues of avoidance and feelings of revenge as these responses are closely related. Avoidance is not a bad response unless the victim can't remove themselves from the wrongdoer. Unforgiving people have a higher level of fear conditioning leading to a fearful response to being wronged. Recalling the hurt takes place in safe, supportive and non-hurtful environment. The victim can vent their feelings of anger, fear, denial, and negative feeling of revenge, hate and anger. Recalling the hurt may take some time as the goal is to change a victim's response from the hurt.

Step Two looks for the wronged to emphasize with the offender. Empathy is the key to Pyramid Therapy. The therapist tries to get the victim to think about the offender and to actually visualize themselves as an offender. How did it feel to be them? What was the offender thinking? Recall a good experience with the offender, or imagine a positive interaction. The therapist should look for feedback clues such as tight facial muscles, rapid beating heart, or other signs of stimulation. If the therapist can garner an emphatic response an emotional modification can take place. Once a feeling of empathy emerges a change can start to take place. Step Three is the process where empathy sees some movement toward forgiveness and the granting of active altruism. Together they move from guilt to gratitude to gift (altruism). They seek a healthy sense of wrong without expecting shame.

Here, the offender may actually start to realize that they harmed somebody. The therapist looks to encourage humility and empathetic identification. Guilt is healthier than shame so a forgiving person will find a release of the hurt and move toward relief. If the wronged gives the wrongdoer the gift of forgiveness emotional changes can occur. Both parties can ultimately find a healthy sense of one-ness emerging. The fourth step is making a commitment to forgive. Without a commitment a fear-conditioned response may result. To move past a possible re-injury the victim needs to make a total commitment to forgive. There needs to be a movement past a victim state of mind. The body and mind work together to modify the state of mind of un-forgiveness to forgiveness. Finally, the victim holds onto the forgiveness. They change their negative feelings associated with the injury. Victims can learn emotion management techniques and focus on their accomplishments rather than failures. In a perfect matrix forgiveness and reconciliation will be I n the same cube. Forgiveness offers a victim a calm openness. Forgiveness is a cure for low self-esteem and it can end deep personal misery. Genuine forgiveness is voluntary and unconditional. It involves the transformation of the forgiver and the forgiven. All involved must be able to receive and give gift of forgiveness. It requires conviction and strength. Forgiveness is not a weakness.

Our personalities may vastly affect the degree to which we are willing to forgive. One method used to assess a person's level of preferred psychological outcomes is known as the OCEAN method. The OCEAN method considers those observable traits about people. OCEAN stands for; O is for openness to experience, C is for conscientiousness, E is for extraversion, A is for agreeableness and N is for neuroticism. OCEAN has been used to predict physical health and psychological outcomes. This five-factor trait analysis is a valuable way to describe people as to their viewpoint. OCEAN offers users a method to consider how people solve problems and achieve goals. The method allows a process to help people tell their life's story. It helps design a pattern of dispositions, personal goals and self-perceptions that really shape the forgiveness possibility.

A forgiving person most likely has a personality trait that leans toward one who has a benevolent attitude and seeks harmony in life. These people are able to manage anger and understand viewpoints of others. They can forgive and receive forgiveness readily. The narcissist, on the other hand, seems to be both normal and pathological at the same time. Narcissists are grandiose, self-loving exhibitionists, defensive and they feel entitled. They exploit others and lack empathy. Unfortunately, they tend to be prominent in Western societies. Our culture is oriented toward personal gratification self-enhancements and authority seeking personalities. Traits such as vanity, explosiveness, entitlement and self-sufficiency are rewarded. The core of forgiveness is empathy, the opposite of narcissism. Narcissism is the natural enemy of the forgiver. Humility is the ability to see oneself as being equal with many other human beings. They can accept differences in beauty, wealth, social skills and intelligence. Humility is free from arrogance. Forgivers are humble and free from the dangers of narcissism. Narcissists seek revenge, they have the capacity to hate people who wronged them and they are powerful inhibitors of forgiveness.

The psychology of forgiveness offers three paths. First, there must be some recognition that harm was done. Then the conspecific congruence must be altered. Second, there must be a commitment to forgive. Thirdly, the parties involved in the forgiveness process must realize that is requires a complex neurocognitive process.

Forgiveness is a behavioral process. It really needs motor and verbal exchanges for it to be complete. The benefit is to emerge from the process with a newly discovered sense of self. Looked at from another point of view, forgiveness is a process that begins with an injury. The brain sense an incongruence and attempts to resolve it. Then, the brain shifts to a higher processing level and a revised sense of understanding of self emerges. Eventually, a reconceived sense of self evolves. The right hemisphere uses its creativity to resolve problems oriented in the concrete/ objective left hemisphere. Once the brain reconciles toward forgiveness, the victim finds they have a lowered heart and respiratory rate, less anxiety, less depression, less hostility and anger and an overall improvement of self-esteem. Forgiveness also improves relationships and helps people to form stronger bonds to one another. Forgiveness and healing go hand in hand. It is difficult to imagine one without the other. Forgiveness is an important phenomenon, physically, psychologically and spiritually.

Chapter 4

Restorative Justice

There are no two wrongs that look exactly alike. Thus the law seeks to objectify the offense in order to bring about congruence. With its rules the legal system tries to correct an imperfect system of revenge with all sorts of clearly defined punishment arrangements. The system wins their argument when the wronged feels as though God blesses the victim and the wronged ends up feeling as though they were part of a normative process with a defined beginning and end. But what about forgiveness and justice? The psychological approach shows us that forgiveness can be considered a gift. Thus, forgiveness can affect justice. Indeed, forgiveness should be part of the justice formula. We know that forgiveness can be step-by-step process (we covered this earlier) and that forgiveness can be taught. Victims can be taught to understand forgiveness. They can be taught to choose to forgive. They can learn to better understand their offense. They can be taught to allow empathy and compassion to grow in their heats. And they can be taught to display their anger. Robert Enright (1998) from the International Forgiveness Institute says, "Forgiveness is the best idea the human race has had since Jesus preached forgiveness."

Forgiveness is a latent construct that is multidimensional and complex. However, it can be more or less observable. Forgiveness is akin to an iceberg where only a bit is exposed for us to see. As in psychology we see forgiveness as letting go of negative feelings toward a wrongdoer. We also seek to obtain, in the process compassion for the offender. Learning to forgive may be the most demanding endeavor for an adult to undertake. But the rewards will be the most meaningful.

In order for it to be meaningful forgiveness requires one to re-live the hurt and reassess the source of hurt while also shifting feelings toward the one hurting you. Forgiveness can be the most transformative experience allowing for the victim to move past selfishness. St. Francis of Assisi prayed, "Where there is hatred let me sow love, where there is injury pardon, for it is in giving that we receive and in pardoning where we are pardoned." We also know that forgiveness is regarded highly in many world religions. It is found in the Hindu tradition some 2500 years ago as they pray, "forgive me all the mistakes I have committed, O lord of love." For the Buddhist, for only love can put an end to hatred. We learn that forgiveness, in the religious tradition, has allowed people to reduce conflict in their lives as well as anger and estrangement. Forgiveness remains as a mainstay of compassion, mercy and humility. But note, seeking forgiveness for yourself with help from a religious person is not the same as seeking forgiveness from somebody that you had harmed. In the religious context, people are seeking forgiveness through God. In the religious context forgiveness is learned through prayer, mediation, instruction and Biblical parables. In Judaism, forgiveness is a obligation. In Tibet, they pray, "remember the good things that you have done, forgive everyone else in your life, and ask forgiveness from anyone you have harmed. In the Lord's Prayer we ask for forgiveness for those who trespass against us.

What about the secular world? The self-help industry pushes scores of publications and videos addressing how to manage shame, guilt, grief, depression and forgiveness. These self-help guides are teaching how one might become slow to anger and let go of anger and resentment. Interestingly, intervention techniques all have forgiveness embedded in them.

Treatments for heart disease, breast cancer, alcoholism and addiction include treatment for forgiveness. Forgiving others can reverse ill health and reduce hostility and inner turmoil resulting in an easing of the work of the heart and an improved immune system. People reporting a forgiving heart also report an ecumenical spiritual intervention. God intervened, they report. Participants in forgiveness intervention programs consistently report less resentment, improved health, less depression and they report that they experience generally reduced anxiety.

The challenge facing criminal justice professionals today is how to engrain the benefits of forgiveness into the justice decision making process. Walters (2015) studies the therapeutic benefits of restorative justice for the stakeholders in homicides. He found that restorative justice programming in England and Wales helped surviving family members better understand the meaning of loss by allowing participants to ask previously unanswered questions. The key to the betterment of participants is the exploration of acute emotional pain experienced by those close to the homicide victim. Restorative dialogue can help the stakeholders find emotional and relational transformations. A restorative dialogue can help homicide victims' family alieve some of the destructive emotional drama associated with a sudden loss from a homicide.

Utilitarian forgivers believe that we should forgive to make the world a better place. They think we should forgive for the betterment of mankind. Certainly, forgiving offers some a feeling of happiness. But many believe that punishment is the best means to balance the balance sheet on the justice scale. What about forgiveness in the justice milieu? Forgiveness requires a moral perspective when assessing it.

The moral aspects pose questions like, do we have a duty to forgive? Is forgiveness a virtue? Is there a specific utility associated with forgiveness? Can we forgive on demand? Perhaps for minor offenses we can forgive readily, but what about serious offenses? What if a victim has to absorb a major loss? The problem with a moral duty to forgive is that we might prematurely be forgiving. Most times a victim needs to work through the forgiveness process. Should forgiveness require a sacrifice? A state of genuine forgiveness should end up being pleasant for both the offender and the victim. The major reason to seek forgiveness is for the betterment of the victim. Forgiveness should never include a sacrifice if lifts the burden of hatred and resentment. Forgiveness and resentment then, need to be assessed on the moral scales leading to the decision process to forgive. Thus, the status of the offender must be weighed. The decision makers are going to have to assess the attitude of the offender. Attitude-based reasons to forgive push the decision into the realm of psychology and attitudes are not easy to morally assess. But, unconditional forgiveness can be appropriate because it responds directly to the offender as a person. It helps the victim as well.

Genuine forgiveness requires a process. Unless the decision makers are held to an agreed upon process, a premature forgiving may take place. A premature forgiving will impact the victim's self-respect which is at the core of genuine forgiveness. It is a fundamental component for both sides. But remember, healing from a victimization is complex and can be idiosyncratic. The process may include a number of tasks beginning with the victims recovering their self-esteem. The victim must regain their self-esteem in order to re-stake their moral status and be on a level playing field with everybody else regarding feelings. The victim must have clarity of mind regarding their worth as a person.

The wronged person must completely understand the nature of the offense and the nature of themselves regarding the incident. The second task is to recognize the wrongness of the act. The victim must recognize how the act committed against them was wrong. The third task is to recognize their true feelings about the incident. During this phase the victim confronts their feelings of grief, anger, betrayal, or any other variety of emotions that may arise. Feelings are critical as many people may shut down their emotions during times of strife. Many times family members (secondary victims) are let out of this process. The victims, in order to respect themselves, must explore the feelings associated with the incident. This has to take place to address the wrong committed against them. The fourth task is to self-assess the situation with the offender. Is there a possibility of harm in the future? Are there significant problems in the relationship? Failure to address these issues at this phase can lead to negative impacts on the forgiveness process, or even worse, negatively impact the victim's sense of self-respect. The fifth task is for the victim to express their beliefs and feelings toward the offender. Here the victim makes a clearer assessment and objectives of the offender. This phase reduces the chances of conflicted expectations and attitudes. The final task is to assess the need for restitution. Respect for integrity may require restitution. If the victim flows the tasks outlined above they will be able to forgive the offender. The victim needs to obtain appropriate levels of self-respect in order for the forgiveness to be genuine. This requires a carefully planned and executed process. If not a premature forgiveness scenario results with can be fatal in a domestic violence situation. Moreover, slavery, oppression and further victimization are worsened by poorly constructed forgiveness plans.

Generally. Forgiveness paradigms fall into one of three categories, unconditional, unilateral or bilateral. The unconditional forgiveness paradigm requires a response form the offender most likely in the form of repentance. In a unilateral forgiveness paradigm the victim unilaterally cultivates their own attitude without any regard for the offender and requires no response for the wrongdoer. The bilateral forgiveness paradigm the victim develops a unique relationship with the offender independent of attitudes from the offender. In a criminal justice scenario the victim may hold onto bad feelings manifested by aversion to forgiveness, but, if the victim sees themselves as a moral person they may consider forgiveness independent of the wrongdoer's actions. This can happen if the wrongdoer refuses to repent and resentment on behalf of the victim can result. When an evildoer really needs forgiveness and the wronged does not give it to them the balance of power remains with the victim. The victim can maintain the upper hand by refusing to forgive. Resentment and rejection can be used to manipulate the wrongdoer. This may lead to an increased sense of the victim's self-wroth. But if we truly respect ourselves then we will never react to the beliefs, actions, and attitudes of others. Again, the goal is to build the self-worth of the victim.

If we live our lives with a true sense of worth then our morality cannot be subjected to harm by wrongdoers. What if the self-valued person feels sorry for the wrongdoer? Can empathy undermine a sense of self-worth? Resentment may serve some people sometimes because sometimes we don't know what else to do when we are wronged. We simply need to react. But instead of fighting we can learn to address the wrong and allow a different perspective to take hold. We can work on creating an objective attitude. Perhaps work on making the offender's actions a new social policy.

We can begin to work on a thing that can be dealt with. An unrepentant wrongdoer is the author of his own wrongful actions. Holding a wrongdoer responsible creates a psychological identification with the wrong (the sin). The offender must meet certain conditions for forgiveness. The wrongdoer, in order to change unforgiving attitude of the wronged, must repent and stop acting like the enjoyed hurting somebody. Both sides need to be aware of connecting the sinner to the sin. If not, this can lead to feelings of resentment. We should try to reframe the offense in such a way as to be able to see the offender as a sentient being and, at the same time, avoid objectifying him. Remember, we seek to not resent the offender.

Resentment toward the offender fosters hostility and decreases goodwill. Unconditional and genuine forgiveness and the associated self-forgiveness are always appropriate. When we determine a person needs punishment we make judgements based upon their actions and we try to connect the punishment to a measure of wrongfulness. This fosters resentment and punishment fosters bitterness. On the other hand, forgiveness, requires respect, compassion and goodwill for all persons involved in a decision regardless of who they are and what they have done. Everybody makes mistakes and everybody deserves to have opportunities for personal and moral growth. Everybody deserves to have a rich-rewarding life complete with appropriate meaning.

A basic moral principle of justice calls for the recognition that no person should be forced to sacrifice any benefit afforded to others so that others can benefit in significant ways. We need a mechanism to keep our justice system in check. A yard stick, if you will, to keep an eye on our levels of compassion, respect and goodwill. We, as a society, shouldn't have to rely upon civil disobedience and demonstrations to measure of levels of fairness in the justice system. Of course a sizable demonstration can have lasting effects and create the need for change. Moreover, we need to make sure that justice extends to all people in every aspect. This means every aspect of due process and the justice system including police, courts, corrections and law makers. We should recognize that each person maintains the capacity to experience happiness, moral choice, growth and awareness. We must learn to identify with people from this perspective. Additionally, we should also learn to identify with people who are living on the margins of society, those left out, homeless or incarcerated. We should create a society where we care deeply for and sympathize with the incarcerated. We should demonstrate our sympathy and care for those suffering the cruelty of prison.

Just Deserts

What about deserts? Deserts has a long history of philosophical tradition and is a component of morality (Holmgren 2012). At least some criminals deserve punishment. At the same time, other offenders deserve treatment. Is the decision point one of intellect, or skill, or originality, or something else altogether? What a criminal deserves can be a difficult thing to sort out. Is the criminal possessing a wrongful or evil heart and mind? How much harm was done? How was the community affected? Desert-ists justify their claims that offenders deserve punishment because punishment is a fundamental principle of their theory. So simple, but so complex! But this theory has little explanatory power. Thus, the greater risk of accidental acceptance by like-thinking moralists. The second thing a dester-ist might claim is that the offender has the punishment coming to him. Criminals expect to get punished. This is their justification.

The problem is that those who get punished deservedly so, and if they are punished in proper proportion to the offense they committed and the attitude amassed against them. If this is the single justification for the punishment, then those who don't misbehave should get rewards to the relationship of the good they do. This is the flaw in the justifications argument.

The justifications for retributive reactions are not morally appropriate. And we should not be morally justified to punishment if other means are available. Can't we figure out a way to sentence an offender without sending him to prison? This is especially a moral question as we now know the detrimental punishment is to the offender. Just because we have used prisons for centuries does not necessarily make it morally right. Prisons have become natural, normal, or even customary in the criminal justice milieu. Even though it has a history, punishing still remains a very much as a reactionary fashion and it does not justify the use of prisons as punishment.

Some argue that virtuous people deserve to do well and vicious people deserve to not do well or to do poorly. But some people who act in a vicious manner have also been victimized. Should they get a pass? Maybe some people simply have yet to develop their virtuosity. Are they lacking virtue due to their immaturity? But, are the virtuous really deserving more benefits from society? The problem remains is just how we are to define are virtuous and how are we to define vicious. How do we decide what is more bad or less bad? What is good? What is less good? But life isn't fair. Some people work hard for their money, some don't. The desperately poor may beg for money or some may never beg. The problem with desert-based models is that it becomes difficult to deliver what is deserved and how do we weigh considerations against other kinds of moral considerations?

To consider a paradigm of justice that includes forgiveness the concept of using people as a means to gain any sort of benefit will be diminished. Plus, adding forgiveness to our paradigm insures that the principles concerned will have secured the most fundamental interests for everybody. Consider what the public expects from the criminal justice system. The public expects crime prevention, restitution for primary harm and restitution for secondary harm. The question remains if the forgiveness paradigm can be tough enough to address the serious and damaging behavior that exists in the world today. Will forgiveness be able to prevent crime and subsequent harm to innocent people and to prevent unnecessary harm to offenders? The idea, in any case, is to prevent crime or other wrongdoing from taking place. To the extent we can prevent crime from taking place we can improve the lives of (would be) victims and offenders. If we include forgiveness in our paradigm non-punitive means will be employed to prevent crime and other harmful behavior. Admittedly, sometimes people steal by stealth or force and sometimes it is justified because the theft does not have the means to sustain a decent standard of living. But, in the forgiveness paradigm, theft is mitigated in acts of desperation. To prevent such theft is a decent standard of living for everybody.

The truth about the science of crime is that most of it causes are correlated with social conditions like poverty, lack of opportunity and the like. If we know this, shouldn't we strive to eliminate the severe social conditions that exacerbate wrongdoing due to desperation? Could science serve to mitigate the severe effects of extreme weather, for example? We acknowledge that severe weather creates desperation and migration of poor people across the globe. Couldn't science serve to address the serve mental health problems in the country with the same intensity as physical illnesses?

Couldn't science work to eliminate the stigma associated with mental illness? We should work to eliminate the stigma and encourage people to seek treatment. As a criminal justice system we could take domestic violence and child abuse more seriously. A forgiveness paradigm will center on violence prevention in the home. There should be guarantees that people seeking help can receive such help. We should be taking stress more seriously. Consider those people who suffer from the greatest amounts of stress. Perhaps by abusive caregivers. Abusive people should be subject to compassionate referrals and intervention programs.

Science in the forgiveness paradigm will be instrumental in reducing stress from bullying and violence in schools. Schools could be models for compassion and respect. The practice of addiction and treatment in and associated with institutions could be much less judgmental. The addicted should be offered clear pathways to treatment. A forgiveness-justice model would take poverty seriously and support effective interventions in poor neighborhoods. Easing racial tensions and addressing unemployment should be a national priority. We need to support all those who collectively found ways to support people living in poverty in a non-judgmental way. Programs need to be developed to stop moral decay and find ways to offer respect and compassion to all people living in poverty. We need to start paying attention to working people who are earning less than a living wage and people who are subjected to ridicule or being shunned. We, as a society need to combat discrimination and offer programs to adults who come from abusive homes, experienced bullying and humiliated at work or school. With that we need to start developing morally appropriate and worthy attitudes amongst ourselves as we start paying attention to our moral standards. Our efforts to be moral should be strenuous efforts. We need to become deeply concerned about those being hurt by moral violation of others. We need to be always moral and good citizens showing the right behavior to all around us. We need to be good examples of effecting change. A change to compassion and goodwill.

Although some people certainly need to be restrained we need to find a way to employ civil commitments to keep citizens safe and neutralize those posing threats to innocent people. These confinements should be done with the least amount of restriction and done in a compassionate way. We need to develop a commitment to forgiveness as a social science and we need to stop layering harm upon harm in the prison system. Suffering causes resentment, self-condemnation, moral censure and retributive punishment. Retribution is not part of the solution. Retribution does not protect people from harm.

Jeremy Bentham (1748-1832) wrote "An Introduction to the Principles of Morals in Legislation." In this book he distinguishes between primary and secondary harm. Primary harm is committed against the victim and secondary harm is that consequence of crime against the community. Our legal system deals with primary harms through tort law (civil law). Torts are actions that are wrong with associated motives such as purposively, knowingly, recklessly or negligently. In law, the wrongdoer is to be held accountable for harms they commit against others and to be forced to compensate the victims for the harm caused. The law imagines an innocent victim. The law ought to see to it that a wrongdoer compensates a victim for losses. Today we put the burden on the wrongdoer, not in the spirit of judgement, but in the spirit of fundamental restitution (as in tort law). The law provides an objective response to a wrong. We don't set limits on how much a wrongdoer is expected to pay. Of course, our laws are codified and sometimes a jury may decide on the amount of restitution.

But even then, the judgement can be appealed. Strict liability can be imposed for those who seek activities that create nonreciprocal harms to others (for profit or fun, perhaps). But what happens when a wrongdoer can't pay the restitution? Today, he receives a prison sentence.

Retributive theories of punishment speak to an imposition of something painful by a person who claims to have the authority to do so on the name of another. Programs of punishment have guidelines. For example no innocent person should be punished, the severity of the punishment must be proportional to the crime committed, and the law must recognize excuses and the punishment must be fair. But fairness can be seen as a weakness. Serious crimes need to be dealt with in a serious manner independent of utility. Like a puppy that needs to be trained. We should punish people to the extent that they need deserve. Most theories of strong retribution are unsuccessful. Simple desert-based theories are those that support the thinking that those who commit a wrongdoing deserve to be punished. These communicative theories suppose that punishment acts as a deterrent and are legitimate. But on the other hand, expressive theories of punishment recognize respect for offenders as human beings and drop feelings of disrespect, hostility and the withdrawal of goodwill. The problem remains unresolved as to how we will pose restitution of a secondary harm or how might we compensate a community for the harm that was committed. The problem remains who is the criminal? What conditions can be repaired? Who receives the restitution? Our court system seems to be overly formal and counterproductive. Judges are hogtied by federal or state sentencing guideless and are deemed in violation (off the grid) if their sentences deviate from the guidelines. The human nature of judging has become lost in the courtroom. What is arising should be restorative justice.

The tenants of restorative justice include the notion that the criminal justice system is about the victim and the offenders. Offenders have the responsibility to compensate the victims. The process of compensation should be negotiated in a non-formal process and the state should get out of the pain delivery business. Restorative justice is not about forgiveness or reconciliation. It is more about choice. There should be no pressure for a victim to forgive the offender or offer reconciliation. Restorative justice is not about mediation either. Victims are not disputants. We want to avoid victim blaming. Restorative justice is more about conferencing. It is designed to reduce recidivism and (or) repeat offending. Restorative justice is the right thing to do. It meets the victim's needs and it addresses the responsibility of the offender. Restorative justice is not a blueprint. Restorative justice is not a map. It is an invitation for dialogue and exploration. It is not necessarily for first-time offenders or minor offenses. Restorative justice is not a panacea or a replacement for the criminal justice system. Restorative justice is not a replacement for jails or prison.

It is not a replacement for retribution. Restorative justice is concerned with the needs and roles of victims and offenders. Restorative justice expands its circle of stakeholders to include the larger community.

Restorative justice focuses on the needs of victims, the needs of the offender, and the needs of the community. For the victims, restorative justice seeks to better collect real information. The objective is to allow the victim to tell their story as the police sort out the truth. The victims also find a sense of empowerment through restorative justice as a return to their former state is sought. The victim additionally has a say in restitution and vindication and they get to partake in a symbolic extraction and receipt of an apology. For the offender, restorative justice seeks to find a level of accountability.

The program brings the offender down to earth and they learn to be less suspicious of the criminal justice system. The offender becomes acutely aware of the process and consequences of punishment in the restorative justice model. They are encouraged to own up to what they did. This allows the offender a chance to alter their wrong behavior and make things right with the victim and the community. The restorative justice model directly addresses the harm, seeks empathy, and transforms shame. Simultaneously, restorative justice models seek community support. Restorative justice seeks change, while encouraging problem solving and employing treatment modalities.

Restorative justice brings a sense of community into the decision making process. The model demonstrates real concern for victims as community members. It builds mutual accountability. Restorative justice restores healthy communications in the community. The criminal justice system holds fast onto notions of just deserts but the restorative justice model focuses on victims, the community and the offender. Restorative justice considers crime as a violation of people (community members) and their interpersonal relationships. To restorative justice proponents violations of the law create obligations. The central obligation is to put things right. Crime represents a wound in the community that tears at the binds and the web of much needed connections between members. The damage done to relationships through criminal acts becomes a cause and effect. Wrongdoing is a sign that something is wrong in a community. Initially, wrongdoing calls for a making it right obligation sitting in the lap of the offender. But the community might have some responsibilities and obligations as well. So, what is required to achieve justice? This is the question that restorative justice programs address.

A new model, in order to work, should support three basic pillars. The three pillars of restorative justice are putting the victim first, the consideration of consequences of wrongful behavior and their corresponding notions of accountability and responsibility and finally, engagement with the stakeholders. The stakeholders are victims, family, friends, and community members, people who care and people from the community looking to change the way things are normally done. The stakeholders in the process form a caring micro-community. The restorative justice model, while managed by a judge or other prominent authority, still maintains inclusive processes and looks to inclusively find outcomes that are mutually agreed to. The outcome is not imposed as a sentence. The problem with a sentence it resembles punishment. And punishment often reinforces the strong sense of victimization for the victim and the offender. The restorative justice model offers communities a way to explore the root causes of crime and the manifest experiences of the victim. Punishment and associated unresolved trauma will be reenacted repeatedly in a traditional court setting. Restorative justice model offer an opportunity to address re-victimization by the criminal justice system. The criminal justice system is poised to punish and quickly stands to deliver even more trauma to the victim and the wrongdoer. But restorative justice encourages outcomes that promote responsibility, reparations and healing for all those involved.

Restorative justice focuses on harms and needs of victims, offenders and the community. It addresses he obligation resulting from the harm. Restorative justice uses inclusive and collaborative processes that include legitimate stakeholders. Restorative justice seeks to put things right. Today we live in a web and we are very much connected to one another in a myriad of ways.

Restorative justice recognized our connectedness and employs a vision of interconnectedness. Restorative justice also recognizes the particularity of people and while striving to be sympathetic to individual needs it equally considers the needs of the collective community. The restorative justice process can particularly remind us that context, culture and personality shape our communities and each are important.

Perhaps most importantly, restorative justice calls respect for all parties involved as well as reaching an appropriate balance of the influencing issues. When we pursue justice in this fashion we do so with respect and restorative-ness in mind. Restorative justice is a process, to the extent possible, designed to bring those with a stake in a specific offense together as to collectively identify and address harms, needs and obligations in order to heal or make things as right as possible. Restorative justice puts decision making into the hands of those most affected by the wrongdoing. It makes healing transformative and it reduces the likelihood of further offending. The process requires the involvement of victims, the offender taking responsibility, the offer to repair the harm, a plan to address the needs of the victim and the community and the real-live capacity to reach closure. Restorative justice is a process by where the community can assess who has been hurt, what are their needs, who has obligations to address those needs, and what is the appropriate process to involve stakeholders in a meaningful manner? The process also finds a way to make things right.

Restorative justice can reduce the negative impact by the criminal justice system on the victim. It helps the stakeholders have a say into the redefinition of the issues and a re-framing of the possible outcomes. The re-framing helps those involved focus more on the harm resulting in the wrongdoing than the rules that were broken.

The process helps the community find a way to show equal concern for both the victim and wrongdoer in the pursuit of justice. The parties work toward restoration and empowerment. Restorative justice supports offenders but encourages them to understand, accept, and carry out their obligations to victims and the community.

The restorative justice process allows stakeholders to find meaningful ways to involve the community in a real problem. It gives attention to unintended consequences of actions and programs. It allows the gathering of stakeholders to show respect for each other. Mutually, the program will seek to address the wrong, restore equity, and assess future intentions. Most important, the restorative justice program diverts offenders away from the detrimental effects of the criminal justice system. The plans can be healing or therapeutic or some plans may offer no diversion for serous wrongdoers. Other programs may offer transitional methods like half-way houses or work plans. Restorative justice programs can vary in degree of restoration form pseudo restorative to non-restorative to potentially restorative to mostly restorative to fully restorative. These programs encourages offenders to take responsibility for their actions and begin new journeys toward transformed selves. These programs are truly designed to change the offender.

Works Cited

Abramson, N. Senyshyn, Y. (2010) - Effective punishment through forgiveness: Rediscovering Kierkegaard's knight of faith in the Abraham story, Organization Studies, 2010 - journals.sagepub.com.https://scholar.google.com/scholar?hl=en&as_sdt=0,31&q=Kierkegaard+God+wants+us+to+forgive

Ammar, N. (2001) Restorative Justice in Islam: Theory and Practice, In The Spiritual Roots of Restorative Justice, Hadley State University of New York Press, Albany, NY

Barett and Berman (2019) U.S, Will Resume Executions, Barr says The Philadelphia Inquirer, July 26

Baumeister, R, Exline, J. and Sommer, K. (1997) The Victim Role, Grudge Theory and Two Dimensions of Forgiveness. In Dimensions of Forgiveness, E. Worthington, Templeton Press, Philadelphia

Bibas, S. (2016) The Decline of Mercy in Public Life First Things: A Monthly Journal of Religion and Public go.galegroup.com

Enright, R. and Coyle C. (1998) Researching the Process Model of Forgiveness, In Dimensions of Forgiveness E. Worthington Templeton Foundation Press, Philadelphia

Girard, R. (1987) Job, The Victim of his People - books.google.com https://scholar.google.com/scholar?hl=en&as_sdt=0,31&q=rene+girard+scapegoat+mechanism+1987

Gull, M. and Rana, S. (2013) Manifestation of Forgiveness, Subjective Well Being and Quality of Life, Journal of Behavioral Sciences, Vol. 23 No. 2 (17-59)

Greely (1995) Cited by Unnever, JD, Cullene, FT and Bartowski, JP (2006) Images of God and public support for capital punishment: Does a close relationship with a loving God matter? Criminology, https://onlinelibrary.wiley.com/doi/abs/10.1111/j.1745-9125.2006.00065.x

Holmgren, M. (2012) Forgiveness and Retribution: Responding to Wrongdoing, Cambridge Press New York, NY

Heufeldt, R. (2001) Justice in Hinduism, In The Spiritual Roots of Restorative Justice, Hadley State University of New York Press, Albany, NY

Huxley, A. (1945) HarperPerennial Books New York

Jones, L. (1995) - Embodying forgiveness: A theological analysis books. google.com https://scholar.google.com/scholar?hl=en&as_sd t=0%2C31&q=Jones+god%27s+love+moves+us+toward+re conciliation&btnG=

Lander, I (2016) Exploring the Place of Forgiveness Therapy in Social Work Practice, Journal of Social Work Practice, Vol. 30, (69-80)

Loy, D. (2001) Healing Justice: A Buddhist Perspective, In The Spiritual Roots of Restorative Justice, Hadley State University of New York Press, Albany, NY

Martin, and Thoresen (1997) Cognitive Models in the Forgiveness Process, in . In Dimensions of Forgiveness, E. Worthington, Templeton Press, Philadelphia

Marty, ME. (1998) - The Ethos of Christian Religion in Dimensions Of Forgiveness: A Research Approach, 1998 - books.google.com

Morton, T. and Postmes (2011) Moral Duty or Moral Defense? The effects of perceiving shared humanity with the victims of ingroup perpetrated harm. European Journal of Social Psychology 41 (127-134)

Singh, P. (2001) Sikhism a Restorative Justice, In The Spiritual Roots of Restorative Justice, Hadley State University of New York Press, Albany, NY

Unnever, JD, Cullene, FT and Bartowski, JP (2006) Images of God and public support for capital punishment: Does a close relationship with a loving God matter? Criminology, https://onlinelibrary. wiley.com/doi/abs/10.1111/j.1745-9125.2006.00065.x

Worthington (1998) In Dimensions of Forgiveness, E. Worthington, Templeton Press, Philadelphia